Rose Summerfield: Australian Radical

Rose Summerfield: Australian Radical

Steve J. Shone

LEXINGTON BOOKS
Lanham • Boulder • New York • London

Published by Lexington Books

An imprint of The Rowman & Littlefield Publishing Group, Inc.
4501 Forbes Boulevard, Suite 200, Lanham, Maryland 20706
www.rowman.com

86-90 Paul Street, London EC2A 4NE

British Library Cataloguing in Publication Information Available

Library of Congress Cataloging-in-Publication Data Available

ISBN: 978-1-66690-940-1 (cloth)
ISBN: 978-1-66690-941-8 (electronic)

Contents

List of Acronyms

AMA	Amalgamated Miners' Association of Australasia
APR	Australasian Pastoralists' Review
ASOA	Australasian Steam Shipowners' Association
ALF	Australian Labour Federation
ASA	Australian Secularist Association
ASL	Australian Socialist League
ASU	Australian Shearers' Union
AWU	Australian Workers' Union
CDC	Central District Council
CIA	Central Intelligence Agency (U.S.)
GLU	General Labourers' Union of Australasia
MAC	Melbourne Anarchist Club
MLA	Member of the Legislative Assembly
MP	Member of Parliament
QLU	Queensland Labourers' Union
QSU	Queensland Shearers' Union
STL	Single Tax League
TOGLA	Tea Operatives' and General Labourers' Association (U.K.)
TUC	Trades Union Congress (U.K.)
TGWU	Transport and General Workers' Union (U.K.)
USS	Union Steamship Company of New Zealand
UPA	United Pastoralists' Association of Queensland
UBI	universal basic income
WSL	Womanhood Suffrage League
WCTU	Woman's Christian Temperance Union

Acknowledgments

An alternative version of chapter 2 was presented in New Orleans, Louisiana, at the 2021 Centennial Annual Meeting of the Southwestern Social Science Association. The author is grateful to Jennifer Brubaker, Bill Carter, Jenny B. Clark, Sam Freeman, Jennifer Horan, Nathan Jun, Aaron King, James D. King, Richard T. Longoria, Howard Price, J. D. Rackey, James Riddlesperger, and an anonymous reviewer for their helpful comments and valuable suggestions for improvement that have allowed him to refine many of the arguments presented in this volume. All errors should, of course, be attributed to the writer himself.

Introduction

This work is the first book-length study of Rose Summerfield (the name which will be used consistently here, although she was originally Rose Stone and later Rose Cadogan, and wrote articles under the name Rose Hummer), the creation of which has allowed the present author to replicate an investigative process that previously resulted in the first extensive portrayal of another radical, though somewhat different thinker, Lysander Spooner, which was titled *Lysander Spooner: American Anarchist* (Shone 2010). Part of the reason why no other longer analysis of Rose has previously been undertaken is likely because there are many gaps in the source material. Fortunately, the fact-finding process in the present case has been aided by tracing the details of Rose and her family and of her later life in Paraguay using newspapers and other publications of the time. That activity has been greatly facilitated by the existence of Trove, the online research database of the National Library of Australia, and, to a lesser extent, Papers Past, the equivalent service of the National Library of New Zealand, as well as Chronicling America, a similar facility that is provided by the U.S. Congress.

Another reason for exploring the life of this original, intellectually sophisticated labor activist, socialist who was sympathetic to anarchist ideas, feminist, secularist, dynamic speaker, and all round radical thinker is that some of the people who have tried to portray her achievements have included significant defects in their accounts. For instance, in his chapter, "The Utopian Diaspora: Australians in Paraguay," Andrew Harvey (2010) claims that Rose and her second husband, Jack Cadogan, moved to South America in 1908, when there is ample evidence that it was actually 1899; he also says that her maiden name was Summerfield, when in fact it was Stone, Summerfield being the name she acquired when she married her first husband, Henry Lewis Summerfield. Although such obvious errors are missing from Mark Hearn's paper, "Rose Summerfield's Gospel of Discontent: A Narrative of Radical Identity in Late Nineteenth Century Australia" (Hearn 2004), which is by far the most essential existent work about Summerfield, unfortunately the title of this generally interesting and informative article reveals confusion between two entirely different speeches that she gave, undermining both the title and the substance of his research. Moreover, both Harvey and Hearn exaggerate the significance of some of the occasional comments that she made about minorities, distorting her point of view. In *Paradise Mislaid: In Search of the Australian Tribe of Paraguay*, an account of the settlers who left Australia and their descendants, Anne Whitehead presents snippets of Summerfield's life that by themselves have the effect of damning Rose with faint praise, such as her comment that "Rose . . . had become quite famous in Sydney as a poet and lecturer on socialism and women's rights" ([1997] 2018, 370). But Summerfield was much more than this.

Chapter 1 explores Summerfield's efforts as a union official and the roots of her commitment to labor activism that lay in the Great Strikes of the early 1890s, focusing on her speeches and the rhetoric she used, and the ways that her eloquence when participating at meetings of various kinds would enthrall listeners and became a vehicle for expanding the reach of the Australian Workers' Union beyond its more likely supporters, as she emphasized the concerns of women and poor people, the unfairness of government, employers, the newspapers, and court officials, and the need for land reform.

Chapter 2 looks at Rose as a women's rights activist. She was one of the leaders of the influential Womanhood Suffrage League interest group in New South Wales (NSW), but although she worked to obtain the vote for women, she remained skeptical that such an accomplishment would help to achieve many of the other societal reforms for which she campaigned, and her disagreements with other feminists of the time raised issues about what kind of changes would suit women of different backgrounds, and what kind of employment would remain inappropriate. She emphasized the need for marriage to become a more personalized institution, giving individuals much more scope to live their lives as they wished.

Chapter 3 looks at Summerfield as a political theorist, discussing her secularism, as well as her sympathies for executed anarchists and the strands of her own ideas that suggest the influence of anarchism. She was also a socialist, who worked for the Australian Socialist League, conferring on them also the privilege of using her skills as an orator, although she did not necessarily commit to every dogma, and she defended the rights of illegitimate children, whom she believed, like women, were entitled to be treated with respect.

Chapter 4 considers the singularity of the rather limited role that Rose has so far been assigned by the academic world, not only because of the restrictive amount of materials that remain available to the present-day investigator, but also because some of the research that does exist contains errors and does not really do Summerfield justice; she was a thinker whose life and work demand greater recognition. It is surely time for a more tolerant understanding of her beliefs, of what she sought, and of what she accomplished, to emerge.

Chapter 5 looks at Summerfield as an emigrant and settler at Colonia Cosme in Paraguay, and the ways that she attempted to deal with the transformation of her life as well as her regret, insofar as it existed, at having left Australia behind. The failure of the New Australia Co-Operative Settlement Association, like so many other utopian dreams that came crashing down in disappointment, perhaps emphasizes how inspired thinkers such as Rose, who are well able to describe all the many problems and examples of injustice that exist in the modern world, find improving the lot of humanity to be a far greater challenge, and an agenda that in the twenty-first century remains largely unfinished.

Chapter 1

Labor Activist

As Hearn (2004, 67) points out, "The only way of biographically approaching Rose Summerfield, and interrogating the connection between her identity and social action, is through a close reading of her surviving texts." Unfortunately, beyond those limited numbers of enduring writings, there is often little to be found about her life, although it is far from impossible to use the fragments that remain to construct a useful narrative. Rose Summerfield (1864–1922) was born Rose Anna Stone in Middleton Creek near Ballarat, a gold mining area in the Australian state of Victoria. Her mother was Mary Stone, who died on March 17, 1897, after a long illness, and her father was John Stone, who preceded his wife in death. Rose had two brothers, named Joseph Stone, who was about four years older than she was, and John Stone. Her first husband, Henry Lewis Summerfield, was a freethinker like herself, whom she married on March 23, 1886; Rose was 21 at the time, while Henry was 55. Henry worked as a tailor, though in October 1864, his self-employment resulted in having to file for insolvency, when his liabilities exceeded his assets by approximately £100 ("Death" 1922; "Deaths" 1897; Hearn 2004, 64, 68, 2005; "Insolvency" 1864; "New Factory Legislation: In Victoria" 1897). He died on March 10, 1890, and Rose was allowed by the NSW Supreme Court to become the executor of his will, replacing the person named on the document, Ebenezer Skinner, the leader of the Sydney affiliate of the Australian Secularist Association (ASA) and publisher of *The Secularist's Guide: A Book for Young and Old* (c. 1890), whose daughter, Alice Annie Skinner, would marry William Whitehouse Collins, who around this time became the president of the Canterbury Freethought Association in New Zealand. Rose married her second husband, John "Jack" Cadogan, a shearers' cook and single tax advocate who edited and drew cartoons for a Sydney newspaper called *The Democrat*, on September 22, 1897. She had five sons: Harry "Enrique" Summerfield, León Cadogan, who was born in Paraguay a few weeks after Rose and Jack arrived there, Eric Wayne Cadogan, Hugh Cadogan, and Bronte Cadogan ("Death of Rose Summerfield" 1922;

"Editor's Note" 1926; Fiedler 2016, 50; Hearn 2004, 78–79; "In the Supreme Court of New South Wales, Ecclesiastical Jurisdiction. In the Will of Henry Lewis Summerfield, late of Waverley, near Sydney, in the Colony of New South Wales, Gentleman, Deceased" 1890; Molesworth 1926; "Notes and Comments" 1897; Stenhouse 1993).

SHEARERS AND MINERS ON STRIKE

Rose Summerfield's substantial involvement in union activity and her eventual decision to emigrate to Paraguay had roots in the Great Strikes of the early 1890s, beginning with the large-scale combined maritime, sheep shearers', and miners' strike, which commenced on August 16, 1890. Merchant marine workers attempted to improve their pay and working conditions, and were supported by other wharf workers, shearers, and miners, resulting in a total of 60,000 employees being out, with additional related action being held in New Zealand, on account of its Union Steamship Company (USS), which did much business in Australia and was a member of the Australasian Steam Shipowners' Association (ASOA), and in Fiji, where dock workers at the Queen's Wharf in Suva, aware of what was happening in Australia and New Zealand, sought a doubling of pay. The use of what one side referred to as "free labor" and the other side denigrated as "scabs" and the subsequent lockout of the Broken Hill, NSW miners meant that the 1890 strike lasted for only sixteen weeks, with the Newcastle, NSW area miners being the last to concede, on November 5. However, more strikes would soon follow, and in 1891, the shearers and then, in 1892, the Broken Hill miners fought their own battles against the same tactic employed by employers, who announced the ending of an existent agreement, which led to conflict ("Back Matter" 2010, 286; Campbell 1945; Merrett 1969, 25–27; Nicole 2006, 140, 140 fn. 64, 2011, 120). Whitehead notes:

> The little Queensland town of Barcaldine, it could be said, was where the whole thing began. The Great Shearers' Strike of 1891 was the forcing ground for the Paraguayan experiment. (Whitehead [1997] 2018, 62)

An underlying factor was the attitude of employers toward unionized and non-unionized employees, as Svensen explains:

> The practice of dissolving unions was not widely adopted in Australia. Employers simply gave preference to non-unionists and intimidated workers who joined or remained in unions. Supervisors were upbraided for dismissing

> non-union hands even when the men concerned were incompetent or drunk. (Svensen 1995, 226)

The shearers' employers, the pastoralists, were large-scale sheep graziers, also known as "squatters," notwithstanding the alternative definition of that word as persons who live on land without owning it, which at one time had applied to many of those who occupied and farmed formerly Aboriginal land. Prior generations of these pastoralists had in the early nineteenth century used criminals serving prison sentences to do the shearing and shepherding work. Now, they responded to a drop in wool prices by cutting salaries and lobbied for more changes using the slogan of "freedom of contract," undermining existing contracts that imposed rates of pay and governed the working conditions of 90 percent of the shearers (Campbell 1945; Laurie 1938, 80, 82–83; Leach 2002, 90; Souter [1968] 2012, 12). The United Pastoralists Association of Queensland (UPA), a group founded in 1890 to counteract the activities of the shearers' unions, issued in 1891 a printed document giving their side of the argument, in which they insisted on the need for "freedom of contract," which they defined as follows:

> "The employer is free to employ whom he chooses, and the employee is free to engage or to refuse to engage to work as he pleases"—which was more fully defined to mean the right of any person to give or accept employment without interference or molestation. (United Pastoralists' Association of Queensland 1891, 3)

Under the aggressive leadership of Orkney Islands-born future member of the Australian House of Representatives, W. G. (William Guthrie) Spence, the era was one of constant mergers of unions in order to improve the strength of labor as a whole. As a leader of the Amalgamated Miners' Association of Australasia (AMA), Spence had started the Australian Shearers' Union (ASU) in 1886, and the rest of the 1880s and 1890s saw its expansion and unification with other organizations, although at times dissident factions sought to break away from the larger unit and return to the constituent component, which had technically now been abandoned; on other occasions, proposed mergers were initially rejected by the membership, such as the failure in 1893 to convince the Bourke, NSW and Wagga, NSW members of the Amalgamated Shearers' Union of Australasia to unite with the General Laborers' Union of Australasia (GLU) (Laurie 1938, 82–83; "Queensland Labourers' Union: Disaffection Among Bush Workers" 1893; Untitled 1893).

The Queensland Bush Workers' Strike Committee issued their own manifesto, signed by their secretary, H. J. Jackson, and the Great Shearers' Strike of 1891 that commenced in January ensued when, following a refusal to sign a new agreement instigating "freedom of contract," strikes of non-union sheds were implemented by shearers across Queensland with the support of the maritime workers who blocked the transit of wool from non-union sources. In their own manifesto, the strike committee delineated the main causes of their dissatisfaction: that new work rules and lower salaries had been introduced without there being any discussion or negotiation with the employees; that the pastoralists had refused to talk to the union unless the principle of "freedom of contract" was conceded in advance; and that there was a conspiracy between the employers and the colonies' governments to deliberately weaken the union movement. In response, the document encouraged workers to oppose the plans of their employers as actively as possible:

> There is no disgrace in being arrested by unjust authority and no cause to fear imprisonment, which is for the sake of a movement which seeks only the welfare of the wage-earners, and through them of all humankind. ("The Queensland Strike" 1891)

In the strike action, shearers were represented by the QSU and the ASU, while less-skilled employees belonged to the Queensland Laborers' Union (QLU) or to the GLU. The withdrawal of labor generated a government overreaction, with police and the military dispatched to quell incidents of strikers setting fire to woolsheds and fences. Union leaders were arrested and imprisoned as, sometimes armed with guns, they attempted to prevent non-union replacements, who were being offered a much higher rate of pay than the one asked for by the union, from reaching the work areas. In response, journalist and Australian Labour Federation (ALF) organizer William "Will" Lane, who was currently the editor of the Brisbane *Worker* and had been attempting to promote inter-union cooperation, wrote his book, *The Workingman's Paradise: An Australian Labour Novel* (Lane [1892] 2005), an inspirational work that would help influence many unionists to relocate to communal life in Paraguay, where he would briefly serve as their leader at the New Australia and then the Cosme settlements before abandoning the project; as he leaves Cosme, eventually settling in New Zealand, Rose Summerfield and her family are arriving at the commune. During the 1991 strike, the ALF was already drawing up plans to send emissaries to Argentina to evaluate the possibility of creating a socialist commune there; the New Australia movement would later decide that Paraguay provided greater potential for the project's success (Campbell 1945; Huf 2010; Laurie 1938, 84–85; Leach 2002, 90; "Queensland" 1891a; Semmler 1969, 76; Souter [1968] 2012, 12–18; Stewart 1972, iv; "The Queensland Strike" 1891). For Isaacs, the message was clear:

> Following the failures of the maritime dispute in 1890, the shearers' dispute in 1891 and the great economic depression of the early 1890s, many in the Australian working class came to the conclusion that Australia would not become a workingman's paradise. Some sought other solutions, such as starting anew elsewhere. In fact, even while the Shearers' dispute was unresolved, there was talk of starting anew in Argentina. (Isaacs 2015)

On the other hand, Hannan suggests that the message may have been more questionable, at least for some of the union leaders:

> [I]t is sometimes argued that it was the utter defeat in the shearing strike in Queensland in May 1891, which prompted these men to turn their attention to a movement which planned to leave Australia. Apart from the fact that a number of them had shown interest in this kind of co-operative settlement *before* the strike defeats, it is significant to note that with the exception of Lane, only [William] Saunders, [Alf] Walker and [Gilbert] Casey went to Paraguay. Certainly W.W. Head, who later helped to found the Labour Party in Tasmania, intended to go, but there is no evidence that [T.J.] Ryan, [Arthur] Rae, [D.A.] Cumming, or [John] Meehan expected to go abroad with Lane. (Hannan 1966, 64)

An editorial in the *Queenslander* portrayed the Amalgamated Shearers' Union leaders as being would-be tyrants and liars, the real conspirators who did not have the interests of their members at heart:

> Can the working men of Queensland, when they think the matter over quietly, give their support to such leaders? Has it ever occurred to them, should the scheme of these men be realised, what might be the fate of any unionist who gave them offence? History is full of stories of the failure of men who have gained power without having been first educated to a knowledge of its right uses. It is full, too, of stories of the overbearing tyranny of such men during the time their brief authority lasted. ("The Bush Workers" 1891)

In the case of William Lane in his role as the leader of the New Australia settlement in Paraguay and on the ship journey there, the editorial seems with the advantage of hindsight to be quite prophetic. But W. G. Spence, though over the years he has had both admirers and critics, seems consistently honest about the nature of the alternative conspiracy, which existed between different employers' groupings, who set out to abandon agreements with labor unions, increasing their profits as they reduced the incomes of those unfortunate to be working for them, under the duplicitously named philosophy of "freedom of contract"—not a liar at all. He was a man with a lifetime of service to the betterment of working people and their lives, even if as a member of parliament he could no longer represent the union interest alone. Lansbury (1967, 3) calls him "the best-known and most widely-respected trades unionist in

Australia." The strikes of the 1890–1894 period convinced him of the need to find a better way to achieve harmony in the workplace, with adequate conditions and remuneration being realized without resort to strikes and their consequences; this included building a stronger union that would be able to use its power and influence to achieve progress (Untitled 1893). However, as Svensen points out, progress did not actually result, even as that union pressure led to the creation of the Australian Labor Party, which might have been expected to bring Spence and other labor leaders' goals to fruition:

> Far from liberating the workers from the yoke of capitalism as Spence had confidently predicted, the parliamentary and industrial strategy of the Labor Party served to reinforce the subjection of workers to capitalism. (Svensen 1975, xiv)

The 1891 shearers' strike ended with workers in some places hungry or with only melons to eat, owing money to retailers, who had mostly now declined to provide credit, while unsympathetic newspaper reports like the one above maligned the union—for example, noting a deteriorating financial situation at the hospital in Barcaldine, which the strike committee, the presumed cause of its supply of patients, had declined to ameliorate ("The Bush Strike" 1891). The lack of funds, partly caused by the only limited amounts contributed by other unions, along with the government's efforts to enable replacement workers to reach shearing areas and continue production, rendered the unions' goals impossible to achieve. A not completely unsympathetic editorial in the *Sydney Mail* argued that the shearers should have anticipated their demise:

> It should be remembered that the Queensland shearers went into this conflict on their own authority, and it is now clear that they miscalculated their own resources and the amount of practical sympathy they would receive. . . . One reason given for the failure of the maritime strike was the amount of surplus labour. This labour was known to exist, and to be available for Queensland bush work. The Queensland strike was ordered with a full knowledge of this fact, and the existence of this surplus labour has been more than ever clearly demonstrated. ("Queensland" 1891b)

The demise meant that strike leaders conceded defeat, admitting the need to return to work, although they avoided acceptance of the "freedom of contract" philosophy (Sullivan and Sullivan 1983, 90). Fourteen of their leaders, members and organizers of the Central District Council (CDC) that had been formed by the QSU and the QLU the previous year, and which had then formally organized the strike, were accused of violating the misdemeanor common law offense of conspiracy—for example, of scheming to persuade workers not to go to work, or conspiring to intimidate non-union employees into joining a union. One of the prosecutors in their trial in Rockhampton

Supreme Court, Virgil Power, claimed "there had been a widespread conspiracy all through the grazing districts of Queensland to prevent free labourers from getting employment in what was a free country, and to prevent the pastoralists from obtaining what labour they pleased" (Virgil Power, quoted in "Supreme Court: Criminal Jurisdiction" 1891a), and that each of the fourteen accused could be shown to have been involved in that plot. Souter ([1968] 2012, 14) notes that "[t]he daily newspapers were unanimous in their support of the pastoralists, and liaison between Government and pastoralists could scarcely have been closer"; meanwhile, as Svensen (1995, 125) points out, although employers and their government supporters tended to exhibit an exaggerated concern about unionists' apparent lawlessness, they were often unwilling to recognize that, by hiring non-union "scabs" with little experience in the positions they took, they were endangering the lives and health of others who worked around them.

In the trial, *The Queen v. George Taylor and Others* (1891), the judge was Justice George Rogers Harding, a man born in Somerset, England, who had an orthodox view of law and was an expert in ecclesiastical jurisprudence, a person whom Bolton and Gregory (1992, 120) refer to as a "scholarly fusspot," but who also, as he presided over the courtroom, served as something of an irritatingly ironic comedian. When one of the accused, William James Bennett, the CDC president, sought to sit at a table in order to take notes on the trial, Justice Harding allowed this so long as he would still be able to see Bennett's face in case he might happen thereby to reveal his guilt, and therefore warning him also to be careful about what he happened to say. When the judge noticed that an incriminating label on a piece of evidence that he had ordered removed was still present in the courtroom, he asked Virgil Power about it, remarking on his own vigilance that "It is a case of put not your trust in Princes nor in Powers" (George Harding, quoted in "Supreme Court: Criminal Jurisdiction" 1891b). The trial lasted three weeks. At the conclusion, following a seven-hour summary of the evidence by the judge, the jury, pointing out several times that they were unlikely ever to agree, with its foreman at one juncture protesting that some of its members had not eaten for 24 hours, was nevertheless each time told to go back and continue deliberations. Harding blustered menacingly, "Perhaps there is some person on the jury who does not know his duty, or perhaps there is more than one or two. Probably you have not understood me" (George Harding, quoted in "The Conspiracy Trial at Rockhampton" 1891; Semmler 1969, 81), thereby inciting members of the jury majority to bully any doubters into unwilling cooperation, in the manner in which some of the shearers had been accused of intimidating non-union "scabs," an approach that brings to mind Lysander Spooner's argument that, in practice, trial by jury, far from being a positive aspect of justice or democracy, actually amounts to being "trial by the government itself" (Spooner [1852] 1971, 9). Having spent 48 continuous hours in the jury room, the panel eventually declared twelve of the men, including Bennett, guilty, acquitting two, and Harding sentenced the twelve to three years' imprisonment (Bolton and Gregory 1992, 117, 120, 122; Demack 1991; Laurie 1938, 87–88; "Supreme Court: Criminal Jurisdiction" 1891a; "The Conspiracy Trial at Rockhampton" 1891; "The Shearers' Dispute: The Rockhampton Trials" 1891). As he announced the sentences, Harding sermonized as follows:

> From the evidence it appears perfectly clear to me that the conspiracy which has been proved against you, and which you appear to have carried on—or your puppets—was planned for the purpose of destroying all things in this colony which value peace and order. (George Harding, quoted in "The Queensland Shearers: Mr. Justice Harding on the Conspiracy Cases" 1891)

An editorial in the *Bendigo Independent* opined that Justice Harding had struck a blow for liberty:

> The heavy sentences inflicted by the judge of the Rockhampton assizes should convey a healthy moral lesson to those in need of it, namely, that in free Australia it is not always safe to preach sedition and revolution. ("The Sentenced Shearers" 1891)

Unfortunately, its writer neglected to suggest a solution to the eternal problem that, denied by your oppressor the opportunity to respond to tyranny or exploitation with calls for insurrection, there may not be any realistic way for you to become free. The unionists ended the strike on June 11, 1891, and reached a settlement with the pastoralists following a conference in Sydney in August (Laurie 1938, 88–89). Following this agreement, some in the United Pastoralists Association came to appreciate the value of improving the conditions under which the shearers were employed, recognizing that they could also benefit from avoiding strikes. The *Australasian Pastoralists' Review* advised its readers:

> The most effectual way to disarm the labour agitators is unquestionably to extend to the employees wise and liberal treatment, and it may be hoped that every pastoralist reading these words will at once bethink himself how he can move towards increasing the material comforts of his hands. If, instead of our having strikes and ceaseless bickerings between capital and labour, the unions of employers took the initiative in such liberal-minded reforms, we might expect to expedite the return of prosperity to these colonies. (*Australasian Pastoralists' Review* editorial cited in "The Bush Workers" 1892)

In February 1893, Spence continued to emphasize the need for unionism to adopt a different approach, no longer looking to strikes, and particularly not to large-scale work stoppages, as a means of bringing about improvements in conditions and pay. However, there would be another shearers' strike in 1894. Following the reduction of wages in 1893 to 80 percent of their prior rates without even consulting the union, the employees decided at the annual conference of what had become the Australian Workers' Union, which now included the Queensland Shearers' Union (QSU) and the Queensland Labourers' Union (QLU), to invite the United Pastoralists Association of Queensland to meet and discuss the many issues that the union believed would be likely to lead to a new stoppage. One of the problems from the union's perspective was the adoption of a system of "reference checking" that enabled the pastoralists to blacklist workers thought to support the union. Despite several attempts to achieve a meeting, however, the graziers' organization kept delaying a consequential response ("Manifesto to Bush Unions" 1894; "Queensland Labourers' Union: Disaffection Among Bush Workers" 1893). In June, the union then announced that it would again strike:

> We have tried to avoid this by doing everything possible, save forfeiting our manhood. That we decline to do, come what will. We therefore appeal to the members of the various branches of the Amalgamated Workers' Union to decline to work for those pastoralists who refuse to give them the undoubted right of a voice in the terms and conditions under which they are asked to engage. ("Manifesto to Bush Unions" 1894)

At Broken Hill back in 1892, in response to a fall in the prices of silver and lead, mine owners made a similar attempt to expand their contract labor system to excavation work in violation this time of an existing agreement with the AMA, a maneuver parallel to those imposed by the pastoralists and again inspired by adherence to the ideology of "freedom of contract," which now earned the ire of stopes workers also concerned to maintain existing conditions and rates of pay, although proprietors of the mines did not advocate "freedom of contract" until resistance by the union had led to a strike. When the owners announced that the existing agreement would end on July 31, they did not say what kind of contract system would be adopted, which led to more suspicion as to their motives, since some approaches would be more disadvantageous to the miners than others. When the owners refused to participate in arbitration, the pressure mounted as they were in turn implored by the miners to meet in order to avoid a strike. When the stoppage commenced, they refused again to meet with the strikers to negotiate an end to it unless picketing ceased, and then refused to say if they would agree to a conference if the union did remove the pickets ("The Broken Hill Miners: A

Strike Impending" 1892; "The Broken Hill Miners' Strike: Interview with Mr. Sleath" 1892; "The Broken Hill Strike" 1892a, 1892b; "The Labor Difficulty at Broken-Hill: Miners' Mass Meeting" 1892).

The failure at Broken Hill once more convinced Spence that striking was an inefficient way to secure adequate pay and conditions for workers, noting that the funds spent on this strike would have been adequate to relocate the miners and their families to farmable land where they could become self-employed and avoid having to toil in the appalling circumstances of their present employment (Untitled 1893).

Another reason for dissatisfaction with the outcome of the miners' strike was that some members of the Broken Hill Labour Defence Committee had received jail sentences that they considered both inappropriate and excessive. Acquitted of more serious violations, miners' leaders were convicted in their trial at the Deniliquin assizes, held far away from the Broken Hill area, where it was thought they might have enjoyed more sympathy from potential jurors, only of conspiracy to prevent others from pursuing their lawful occupations. In announcing the sentences, Judge Alfred Paxton Backhouse averred that "by the verdict of the jury you are practically made accessories before the fact to these acts of violence, and I will punish you for that" ("The Miners' Strike at Broken Hill" 1892), even though the jury's acquittals of the accused on charges of fostering social discontent and creating mayhem might have appeared to a reasonable person to render Backhouse's comment contradictory. The most egregious of the punishments were those given to the AMA secretary and leader of the strike committee, Richard Sleath, and to William John Ferguson, also a member of the strike committee; they each received a sentence of two years in prison at hard labor. When Sleath was interviewed by the press at the end of July, he had confidently claimed that the union pickets were doing no harm:

> If the pickets are giving offence to anyone, they might be taken away. No one has ever said that they would like to have them withdrawn; and as they are quiet and law-abiding, and interfere with no one, I do not see how they affect the question at issue. (Richard Sleath, quoted in "The Broken Hill Miners' Strike: Interview with Mr. Sleath" 1892)

However, during the sentencing phase of his trial the following October, another reporter noted how much the union leader's demeanor had changed:

> Sleath wore a fierce scowl. His jaunty, confident air had quite disappeared. He was a literal exemplification of the phrase, "looking black." ("The Miners' Strike at Broken Hill" 1892)

At the same trial, Herman Heberle and John Bennett (his last name is also given as being Bennetts) received sentences of nine months (of which he served six) and three months respectively for assaulting non-union workers, while John W. Don, a non-union employee who had assaulted a picket, was merely bound over to keep the peace ("Mr. Herman Heberle: His Release from Gaol" 1893). An editorial in the *Windsor and Richmond Gazette* argued that the discrepancy between the sentences of, on the one hand, Heberle and Bennett, and on the other, Don, "proves that the dispensers of "law" are very lop-sided in their ideas of Justice" ("The Broken Hill Prosecutions" 1892). At a union meeting on Tuesday, November 8, 1892, after he had thanked Rose Summerfield for her motivational speech, Wagga, NSW-area ASU secretary W. W. Head pointed out that the various convictions meant that "Riot without conspiring and you will only get a few months" ("The Workers Union of N.S.W." 1892). The Sydney *Evening News* saw the harsh sentences as giving greater potency to the arguments of organized labor, including the belief that picketing should receive more legal protection:

> Had Mr. Sleath and his companions got, say, six months apiece, they would have served out their time, would have had a sense of whatever errors they had committed brought home to them, and could not have posed with any great effect as martyrs. ("The Broken Hill Sentences" 1892)

Overacker sums up the situation following the failure of the strikes in this way:

> With falling overseas markets and a reservoir of unemployed non-unionists to draw upon, the outcome was inevitable: the strikers were decisively beaten. It was a fight in which the workers felt that they had been unfairly beaten because those whom they had trusted had turned the strong arm of the state against them. At every critical juncture the troops had been on hand to protect the employer and the non-union "rat," and the "liberal" premiers, whom labor had been supporting, had called out the troops against them. With a sense of grievance came greater solidarity. Taunted by the press during the strike with "Don't Strike—Vote," they accepted the challenge literally. (Overacker 1949, 679)

Moreover, the eventual triumph of the "Don't Strike—Vote" tactical revision in the form of support for the newly created Australian Labor Party soon seemed a hollow achievement, at least for many of the more radical union members who now saw only their more limited goals being fulfilled. Svensen writes:

> Out of their crushing defeats in the 1890s workers scored a victory, but not the victory usually suggested—the creation of the Labor Party, arbitration and the welfare state. . . . Workers had shown that their usual placid and reasonable

> nature did not mean that they would simply lie down and meekly accept the slavery of freedom of contract. (Svensen 1995, 235)

A meeting on Friday, November 18, 1892, at the Protestant Hall on Castlereagh Street in Sydney, was chaired by Rose Summerfield, who endorsed the development of the new, larger organization, the Australian Workers' Union (AWU), which was being created by the expansion of the current General Workers' Union of which W. G. Spence was the general secretary. Spence also addressed the meeting, declaring the modified union's intent to enroll as many new, currently unaffiliated workers as possible, with the goal of avoiding strikes. Both Spence and Summerfield spoke of the value of cooperation with fellow workers, whose strength in numbers would eventually earn the respect of employers. Partly to secure expansion of the membership among female workers, Summerfield now became the organizer of the AWU's women's division ("Australian Workers: New Labour Organisation" 1892). For Rose, that appointment was a sign that men had finally recognized that women had been treated badly in the past, had lacked access to education, and also were no longer to be rejected as "only a woman" (Summerfield 1892c) to whom sweated, repetitive labor could allowably do damage over time to their bodies:

> The Australian Workers [*sic*] Union is to be an accomplished fact. Just picture the good that must result when all workers embracing skilled and unskilled labor of both sexes are united. Strikes against sweating in narrow, dirty lanes, in ill-ventilated rooms, and lots of other bad things attached, won't be failures. (Summerfield 1892c)

A woman who had attended an AWU social in July 1892 wrote a letter to the union-owned newspaper, the *Hummer*, to indicate her satisfaction with what Rose was doing:

> Mrs Summerfield gave a short address, which made Sis. and I feel soft one minute and mad the next. Anyway, the Women's Division of the Australian Workers Union will be a mighty force in the near future. (Smith 1892)

One way that this hope was accomplished can be seen in the way that, in her new role as an organizer, Summerfield was able in August 1892 to work with the leaders of the Boot Machinists' Union as their members became integrated into the AWU. Together with a committee comprised of the boot machinists' president, J. Taylor, and members G. Brown and A. Porter, Rose was able to persuade other bootmakers to join the AWU, a project that the union leaders viewed as resuscitation of existing arrangements ("Trade Affairs" 1892; "Trades Movements" 1892a, 1892b).

MASTER AND MAN . . . AND A NEW WOMAN

On July 17, 1892, Rose Summerfield gave her lecture on "Master and Man." The title may have come from Émile Zola's account of poor, struggling coalminers in northern France in his novel, *Germinal; or, Master and Man*, which has sometimes been translated with just the one-word title, *Germinal* (Zola [1894] 2005). Rose was noticeably literate, wrote poetry, and at times referred to the works of Shakespeare, Shelley, Walt Whitman, and other stars of the canon of literature in the English language, and apparently named her son León after Leo Tolstoy (Whitehead [1997] 2018, 608, 816). Since the conditions faced by the fictional French miners and their families, whose story was partially influenced by what Zola saw when he visited the strikers at the Compagnie des mines d'Anzin in northern France in 1884, were also similar to those experienced by the Broken Hill strikers, as were the solutions proposed by their respective union organizers, it is likely that she would have wanted to read *Germinal*, which was published in 1885, although the book's complete, unexpurgated translation into English by medical doctor, feminist, and eugenist Havelock Ellis did not appear until 1894. However, by 1887, it was already present on a listing of banned books, and Melbourne-based anarchist W. C. Andrade witnessed a customs official seizing copies of it, though it is not clear whether or not they were printed in French, or if they were of the earlier heavily censored English version of translators Henry and Ernest Vizetelly, who had removed descriptions of sexual matters and of the mutilation of the corpse of a storekeeper, the penis of whom starving strikers exhibit on the end of a stick (Zola [1894] 2005, part five, ch. VI). Having encountered an incident of its suppression by government, Andrade was inspired to read the work, and his review of it soon appeared in the Melbourne Anarchist Club's journal, *Honesty* (Andrade 1887, 16; Jullien 2005, xxxi-xxxiii; Petrey 1969, 56). In Andrade's article, he identifies the motive of Zola as follows:

> Monsieur Emile Zola's aim . . . is to foreshadow the healthy fruition of that section of humanity which, like 'the sower's seed,' labors silently for the good of others in the bowels of the earth. (Andrade 1887, 16)

As Andrade points out, the story, which extols the virtues of the men and women, rather than of the masters, involves attempts by the miners to unionize, retaliation against them by the mine owners, and eventually a plan to import workers from outside the area, in this case from Belgium. As was noted earlier, these are all events that occurred in Australia in the early 1890s, involving maritime workers, shearers, and miners, whose existing union contracts were upended by employer attempts to impose "freedom of contract":

> It is a faithful picture of the relation between Master and Man, and points out with philosophic certainty the coming struggle for real independence that is manifesting itself—the struggle for liberty, for ANARCHY. (Andrade 1887, 17)

In *Germinal* are integrated subtly the ideas and exemplars of Mikhail Bakunin, Pierre-Joseph Proudhon and his work, *The Poverty of Philosophy*, Karl Marx, the International Workingmen's Association (IWA, also known as the First International), and a kind of liberation theology, and Andrade sees in the novel's hero, Étienne Lantier, an amalgamation of two different political philosophies, anarchism and socialism (Andrade 1887, 17), although to argue thus is to disagree with the opinion of Cirillo, who contends that the most obviously anarchist character in Zola's work, the Bakunin-like Souvarine, "is characterized by implacable heartlessness, courting universal cataclysm as narcotic against his pain" (Cirillo 1977, 252), and that therefore the message of *Germinal* is never an anarchist one. As will be discussed in chapter 3, it can be maintained that both influences, anarchism and socialism, are embedded in the ideas of Rose Summerfield, who throughout her adult life experienced and argued on behalf of a growing desire for freedom and self-determination that eventually motivated her and others to leave Australia and go to live in Paraguay.

At the beginning of her speech, "Master and Man," Rose distinguishes between the masters she is going to talk about, the owners of businesses, the people who pay others for work, and the men and women who are the wage-earners, the ones who do the actual labor. She compares the economic situation in Australia with the condition described by Shelley (1819) in "Masque of Anarchy" (original title; later cited as "Mask of Anarchy"), one that calls for the people to seize power. "The labor market is glutted: men are walking about helpless and homeless, ragged and breadless" (Summerfield 1892b, 3). Nonetheless, despite the suffering and starvation, the relationship between masters and men and women remains that "ye can go on sowing—they will do the reaping: ye can find the gold and the silver[,] *they* will use it, *they* will store it, *they*, not you will spend it" (1892b, 3). This brings to mind the scene in Zola's *Germinal* when mineworker delegates, concerned that they and their families will no longer be able to afford to eat bread every day, visit the general manager's house to complain about the imposition of a new system of compensation on them which they are sure will result in a two-centime reduction in what they receive per tram of coal that they produce. When he talks with delegates, the unsympathetic manager, Monsieur Hennebeau, has just left his coffee to go cold at the end of a lunch that has included sausage, eggs with truffles, trout, roast partridge, Russian salad, crab, apple-Charlotte meringue, pineapple, grapes, pears, Champagne, and Rhine wine (Zola [1894] 2005, part four, ch. II).

In her version of "Master and Man," Rose emphasizes the creation by workers of surplus value, the profit that employers make from the labor of their employees, a concept that has theoretical significance for Marx and some other economic theorists, and the speech could be interpreted as being more Marxian in its analysis than "The Gospel of Discontent," an address she will give a few months later (and one that, as will be explained, has been confused with "Master and Man"), where the phrase "surplus labor" occurs, but where she is using those words not to refer to profits but to the presence in Sydney of many unemployed; however, in that other speech, as in "Master and Man," she provides an apparent understanding of "false consciousness" that also suggests some familiarity with the writings or ideas of Marx or of his disciples ("Mrs. Rose Summerfield: 'The Gospel of Discontent'" 1892). For Summerfield, ordinary workers in Australia have been cheated of most of the money they earned, because it took the form of profits and was thus spent by the capitalists who employed them; for her, this amounts to "robbery" (1892b, 4):

> You earned hundreds and hundreds of pounds during this lifetime: you got paid a portion of it, a very small portion, the princely sum of 25s. to £2 a week. This was your share. And you took it, and were thankful, whilst your masters, your self-constituted owners. pocketed the thousands that you had earned: they reaped the golden harvest. (Summerfield 1892b, 4)

And yet, Rose protests, most people generally accept this situation, and do not complain about it, even though that acceptance means that most employees will live their lives without the basic necessities of life: decent housing, good food, and the kinds of clothing they wish to wear. There is a sense here of the modern argument that all people are entitled to have their essentials provided, which increasingly today takes the form of a plea for universal basic income (UBI), regardless of the role, if any, that a person happens to play in the unpredictable economy. Also, she is sure, no one should be obliged to work more than eight hours per day, a protection that had only been won at this point in a few industries, and applied selectively. Children, "twelve or thirteen years of age in a close, dusty factory" (1892b, 4). should not be working at all, which they may be at present only because employers refuse to follow the laws, but should instead be allowed to develop at home (1892b, 4, 7). She condemns those who have chosen to employ "delicate children for a few shillings a week [who] took the place of tradesmen and tradeswomen, and . . . had their childishness and innocence crushed out of them by being forced to mix with depraved, vicious creatures working near them" (1892b, 7).

Since everyone has a right to having their fundamental needs met by society, the solution for Summerfield is that everyone should just insist upon having them and take them: they should make it impossible for employers and others to resist workers being given them, and this could be achieved with labor union leadership and the education they will be able to provide (5, 10):

> [I]t will be the gigantic efforts of lion-hearted men, of brave, unflinching women, who will show you the way to gain the produce of your toil. The very thought of so much good fortune almost affrights you. You think so much work can not be accomplished. But I say it can and will. We will force it to a conclusion. We will not lay down our arms till this work be an accomplished fact. (Summerfield 1892b, 4)

She mentions here the "New Unionism" (1892b, 5) that is developing in Britain and New Zealand at the same time, moving beyond the tactic of work stoppages that have caused misery to strikers on occasion, and using cooperation to build an alliance that can overwhelm the opposition.

> Trades Unionism is one good step in the right direction, but it is only one. There is much to be accomplished after its labors have ceased. It must merge into the New Unionism that is being made known to you now by men who are earnest, noble workers in the Cause of Labor. We must all unite together. It is for the common good. Men and women must co-operate, must band together. (Summerfield 1892b, 5)

People who are more financially comfortable also suffer from the inability to apprize the true nature of industry and poverty in Australian cities. When workers are given a day off and head for the beach to enjoy a moment in which they can do as they please and find a little enjoyment, others view them as living a similar existence to themselves, notwithstanding the oppressive work conditions, lack of adequate nourishment, and other disadvantages that are well-hidden from their view. Such moments of recreation not only convey a false impression to more affluent outsiders, but the brief relief they give to otherwise hard-pressed laborers prevents them from collapsing and giving up the fight to survive, which would undermine capitalist production (Summerfield 1892b, 7). From a Marxian perspective, its roots lying in Marx's concept of ideology, this would be "false consciousness," a misunderstanding of their role and place in society (Eyerman 1981, 43, 55), but to Summerfield, who in her address twice quotes Shelley, the philosophical anarchist poet, and at times expresses her sympathies for an anarchist perspective (a topic that will be explored later in the book) the standpoint of Alexander Berkman is also appropriate to mention here. From his prison cell in the Western Penitentiary of Pennsylvania, where he is serving a fourteen-year sentence for the attempted murder of industrialist Henry C. Frick, he reflects upon the mind-set of his fellow prisoners and of others beyond the institution's walls:

> It is a Herculean task to rouse Apathy to the sordidness of its misery. Yet if the People would but realize the depths of their degradation and be informed of the means of deliverance, how joyously they would embrace Anarchy! Quick and decisive would be the victory of the workers against the handful of their despoilers. (Berkman [1912] 1970, 225)

Yet, this does not happen, and revolutionary outbreaks are rare because "[t]he blind mole perceives only the immediate" (225).

Summerfield emphasizes the dangers inflicted upon people when they become old and are no longer able to work their way out of financial distress. At present, there are very few resources available for the indigent aged to access, and many of the facilities that do exist, such as the workhouse, require a humiliating process by which the applicant must prove his or her own condition of abject poverty, even though the pain and disease that now burden them were often created by decades of slavery for others which was always chronically underpaid. Just as the position of working people can best be managed by a labor union that represents as many persons as possible, so much of capitalism should remain in the hands of the state, controlling the economy and the norms under which people labor ("Man and Master" 1892; Summerfield 1892b, 4, 5, 11). At her most socialist here, she extols government as the protector of ordinary workers:

> Let the State be Paymaster; let every man, every woman, every child, be under its protection, then the word master, as we know it now will be an empty sound. (Summerfield 1892b, 11)

Rose turns also on the banking industry, which, she says, purports to work on behalf of its clients, but which is ever ready, at a moment of customer ill-fortune, to turn the tables and hit him or her with extra charges and higher rates of interest (1892b, 6). As is often the case, she identifies a societal problem here that is largely, in the twenty-first century, though technologically updated, at root unchanged, with the substantial profits of a global financial services industry relying on a variety of details in small print, late charges, extra fees, and property seizures to achieve its success.

Fortunately, however, Rose tells those listening to her, help, in the form of a newly energized labor union and a greater, more widespread awareness of the true nature of the way society is organized and the reasons for the persistence of most workers' exploitation and suffering, is now at hand, and a militancy is abroad that will finally oblige them to act (1892b, 10):

> But all is not stagnation—all is not apathy. There is an undercurrent at work in your midst of volcanic heat, volcanic power. The old order of society, and State, home and Government, will be disembowelled in the eruption that is sure to follow when the necessary elements coalesce. The kindling is there already—the fuel is dry. All that is wanting is a spark from the torch of Reason and Right to start the flame. (Summerfield 1892b, 10)

It is not difficult to find similarities between Rose's "Master and Man" speech and Zola's version, in which the latter similarly illustrates the fate of aged workers and announces the revolution that is now afire:

> But the miner was no longer an ignorant brute, crushed within the bowels of the earth. An army was springing up from the depths of the pits, a harvest of citizens whose seed would germinate and burst through the earth some sunny day. And they would see then if, after forty years of service, anyone would dare to offer a pension of a hundred and fifty francs to an old man of sixty who spat out coal and whose legs were swollen with the water from the cuttings. (Zola [1894] 2005, 265)

When she delivered "Master and Man" at Leigh House on July 17, 1892, Rose "was frequently interrupted by bursts of applause, and at the conclusion of her lecture was accorded quite an ovation" ("Man and Master" 1892), but otherwise she was "listened to with breathless silence by an immense audience" (Tui 1892), and it was clear to journalists who witnessed the speech that they were in the presence of a dynamic orator, of someone with sureness and leadership promise. For Tui, Rose's future seemed certain: "Mrs Summerfield is to organize the Women's Division of the Australian Workers Union, and we can confidently say that success is assured" (Tui 1892). Leigh House, in Castlereagh Street in Sydney, was often the location where socialist and other radical speakers could be heard. Later, Harry Holland, born in New South Wales and a former member of the ASL, now a New Zealand M.P. and the leader of the Labour Party there, would recall "the strenuous days of the late 'eighties and early 'nineties of the last century, and the little group of 'extremists' of every shade of militant thought who foregathered at Leigh House" (Holland 1920):

> We were a mixture of Social Democrats, State Socialists, Christian Socialists, Anarchist-Communists, Philosophic Anarchists, Republicans, Single-taxers, and the rest. Most of us were either Australian or British-born, but we included the nationalities of the world. (Holland 1920)

GOSPEL OF DISCONTENT

Almost three months after her "Master and Man" speech, on October 3, 1892, Summerfield delivered another important address, which was called "The Gospel of Discontent." Unfortunately, current scholarship renders these two completely different pieces of oratory as having been the same discourse, but with interchangeable titles. The roots of the misunderstanding can be identified from Mark Hearn's footnote to his important article, which says:

> In September 1892 the *Worker* advertised that Rose would speak in the western NSW town of Bourke on 'Master and Man or the Gospel of Discontent.' (Hearn 2004, 80, fn 2)

Out of this somewhat ambiguous announcement, Hearn understandably comes to the incorrect conclusion that the more famous speech was repeatedly given, and that it had two names. He writes that Summerfield "described herself as 'spreading the gospel of discontent,' a title she used interchangeably with Master and Man for her lesson on radical agitation" (Hearn 2004, 65). However, it seems that what really happened was that, at the time the Wagga, NSW *Worker* advertisement was posted, its author was unsure on which occasions Rose would be performing "Master and Man" and on which nights of her schedule, if any, it would be "The Gospel of Discontent" and whether or not just one of them would take place. A correct reading of the advertisement, therefore, the full version of which (with its additional punctuation, including a semicolon) is: "Mrs. Rose Summerfield, Organizer for the Women's Division of the Australian Workers" Union, will deliver Lectures in Drew's Hall, Bourke, on MONDAY and TUESDAY, OCTOBER 3 and 4, on "Master and Man"; or, "The Gospel of Discontent," and "The Necessity of Woman Organization." Admission Free" ("Mrs. Rose Summerfield" 1892). In other words, on any particular night, one of the first two named speeches or the other might be given. In fact, if you went to listen to Rose speak, what you heard could be any of the three possibilities that were specified. A similarly ambiguous advertisement had appeared a couple of weeks earlier in the Bourke area paper, the *Western Herald* on September 10, 1892:

> We learn that on the evening of the 3rd of October, in connection with the Eight hour demonstration, Mrs. Rose Summerfield will lecture on "The Necessity of Women's Organisation," and "Master and Man, Present and Future," or "The Gospel of Discontent." ("Local & General" 1892)

Consequently, the title of Hearn's paper "Rose Summerfield's Gospel of Discontent: A Narrative of Radical Identity in Late Nineteenth Century

Australia" is rendered inconvenient to its purpose, since it focuses on "Master and Man," and does not discuss any of the content of "The Gospel of Discontent."

Due to the importance of Hearn's otherwise hugely informative article in demonstrating to readers around the world the significance of Rose Summerfield's ideas and actions, Wikipedia's English-language article on "Rose Summerfield" is similarly misleading, and says "In *Master and Man*, which she also called 'the gospel of discontent,' she described the respective places of employer and workers under colonial capitalism, and how that would change if rights were afforded to workers" ("Rose Summerfield" N.d.). But the speech she delivered on October 3, 1892, "The Gospel of Discontent," is completely unlike the "Master and Man" performance she had given on July 17 of the same year, and which was then released as a pamphlet by the *Hummer*. We know this because, on October 5, the *Western Herald*, two days after her presentation of "The Gospel of Discontent," published a very extensive, apparently largely verbatim, account of what she had said—the newspaper wrote that "[t]he lecture was too long for publication in its entirety, but the following are portions of it" ("Mrs. Rose Summerfield: 'The Gospel of Discontent'" 1892). Also, a woman who had attended Rose's performance of both "The Gospel of Discontent" on Monday, October 3, and of "The Necessity of Woman Organization" on Tuesday, October 4, wrote a letter to the *Western Herald* that was published on October 15, disagreeing with the way that another paper, the *Central Australian*, had characterized the presentations as examples of "anarchical and socialistic old women's meetings" ("A Woman Who Heard the Two Lectures" 1892). The Monday performance was chaired by local M.P. Hughie Langwell, who had been elected to parliament the previous year. It does not appear to have been the first time that "The Gospel of Discontent" appeared: an August 23, 1892, meeting of the Australian Socialist League (ASL) at Leigh House decided that Rose would give "The Gospel of Discontent" speech there on Sunday, August 28, and advertisements for it appeared in the Sydney papers: in the *Evening News* on the Friday before and in the *Australian Star* on the Saturday. However, Summerfield's own report of the event in the "Our Sisters' Column" in the *Hummer* gave the day of the presentation as having been Saturday, August 27 ("Australian Socialist League" 1892b; Campbell 1945; "Socialists—Mrs. Rose Summerfield" 1892; "SOCIALIST Sunday Evening Lectures" 1892; Summerfield 1892i). In fact, Rose apparently recounted her own performance, writing:

> The lecturer showed pretty conclusively that the only gospel that had ever done much good for the great mass of mankind was that of discontent. A large and appreciative audience evidently thought so too. (Summerfield 1892i)

When Summerfield became active as a union official, campaigns to limit the workday to eight hours had been underway for a long time in many countries, achieving only limited success around the world. In Australia, the Eight Hours League had been campaigning for that goal in Melbourne and Sydney since 1856, progressing following a work reduction victory for stonemasons in Melbourne that was led by a Welsh-born Chartist, James Stephens ("Eight Hour Day Monument" 2021; O'Lincoln N.d.; Sparrow and Sparrow 2001). However, the movement had so far achieved most of its victories only in the construction industry and, as Bowden (2011, 54) points out, "only a tiny minority employed by the larger building contractors initially received the shorter day." Because of its connection with the Eight Hours protests, October 3, 1892, was designated "Eight-hour night," and on that evening, Summerfield presented "The Gospel of Discontent" at Drew's Hall in Bourke, NSW. On August 1, her service as the organizer of the AWU Women's Division had begun, and she had also been appointed to serve on her visit to Bourke as an emissary for the ASL. While there, she succeeded in starting up a women's local union branch; Burgmann (1985a, 50) notes that Rose "spoke at a meeting in Bourke on the aims and activities of the ASL, after which 29 people joined the ASL and appointed a committee to arrange the future meetings of the new branch." She became thus the first woman to appear on a public stage in that area. Arriving by train, she disembarked into the sweltering environment and immediately sensed the harmful effects inflicted upon those who toiled there out west far beyond the comforts, such as they were, back in Sydney. "I just wonder people don't revolt at being compelled by circumstances to dwell away out here hundreds of miles from a glimpse of the blue sea," she complained, "and in an atmosphere bordering on the mythical heat of Hades" (Summerfield 1892f). During her visit, there were sports events and a parade of many different types of unionists through the streets of the town to celebrate the Eight Hour Day ("Late Country News" 1892; Paroo's Offsider 1892; Scates 1990, 57; Summerfield 1892f; "The Labor Deserters" 1892; "The Socialist League" 1892).

She began the speech by apologizing for its title, saying that she hoped its content would dissipate any nervousness so far engendered. Although many people find amusing the straits into which some of the poor find themselves from time to time, they should realize, Rose points out, that many others are at risk of a similar downfall:

> My heart filled with a great pity when I thought of the poor toilers in the workshops, the factories, the mines and coalpits; when I pictured them, as they in truth are, helpless and abandoned. Why, you ask, how? Don't they work? Don't they eat and drink, and live? Yes, I'll admit all that; but what do they eat and drink, and how do they live? And, further, through the power and oppression of

> capitalistic tyranny, how long are any of you sure of being let live like decent, rational human beings, and the laugh is still against you, ye poor, helpless workers. ("Mrs. Rose Summerfield: 'The Gospel of Discontent'" 1892)

Though the content of "The Gospel of Discontent" is dissimilar to that of "Master and Man," the attribution to the masses of what might be considered to be false consciousness is, as noted earlier with respect to "Master and Man," also present here. Workers are often fooled by moments of economic improvement into viewing their lives in terms of their best moments and memories:

> A few years ago it was a little more possible than now, a wave of prosperity was passing over Melbourne and New South Wales, workmen were in demand, wages were a little bit decent, country wanted opening up, railways had to be built, small manufactories were springing up, mines full of wealth had to be started, of course houses had to be built. ("Mrs. Rose Summerfield: 'The Gospel of Discontent'" 1892)

Because of this widespread presence of misunderstanding, of delusion, a situation much more common before the recent growth of discontent, there is a consequent failure to see that the damages caused by economic downturns are mostly paid for by those least able to afford a reduction in pay, while the capitalists who run the economy are still able to maintain a very high standard of living. People like to see themselves as being successful, and fail to realize that most of them are "just one step above being homeless," mocking the ones who have become the victims of life on the edge ("Mrs. Rose Summerfield: 'The Gospel of Discontent'" 1892). Without development of the healthy feeling of discontent that she advocates, therefore, people will remain unaware of the fundamental unfairness in society, and fail to work to improve their situation:

> If discontent had not been aroused in you[,] you would not have minded it a bit; you would have gone on without a murmur whilst life lasted, slaving and toiling for what you could get, and if you cannot, or will not, spread the doctrine, mark my words, workmen, your lives will be still harder, your work more laborious, your hours of labour longer, and your rate of wages less. ("Mrs. Rose Summerfield: 'The Gospel of Discontent'" 1892)

In lamenting the reluctance to come to judgment displayed by many when considering the collateral damage inflicted upon ordinary people due to the way that society is presently organized—for instance, failing to enquire "about the unfortunate ironworkers who earn the riches for inhuman wretches like [wealthy industrialist Andrew] Carnegie, the author of triumphant democracy; unfortunate men, whose manhood is crushed and destroyed in their efforts to gain their miserable livelihood" ("Mrs. Rose Summerfield: 'The Gospel of Discontent'" 1892)—Summerfield takes the opportunity to note the interrelationship between the harshness of capitalism and the so-called democracy with which it has often been associated and confused. Since her time, it should be noted, the confusion is often applied deliberately by cynical politicians anxious to frame their activities in the most positive light, and it is frequently casually accepted without much reflection by many political scientists. As noted later, Rose's position will cause her to doubt the importance of giving females the vote, a reform to which she dedicated much of her energy in New South Wales, nonetheless at the same time repeatedly emphasizing that by itself, voting would likely achieve little in the way of real social change.

While the expanding feeling of discontent will be valuable in bringing about improvements, it is also a signpost that the exploitative nature of capitalism has been growing worse:

> I see in America, in England, all over the continents of Europe and Australia thousands and thousands of workmen becoming more and more dissatisfied with their surrounding conditions. I see millions of toilers, of every nation looking toward the future with a sickening dread. ("Mrs. Rose Summerfield: 'The Gospel of Discontent'" 1892)

In "The Gospel of Discontent," to the extent that Rose is discussing false consciousness, she can be considered a follower of Marx, but, as was noted, a rival interpretation of the phenomenon lies in the words of Alexander Berkman. Moreover, the way in this discourse that she laments the lack of leisure due to exploitation by capitalism is more like Peter Kropotkin, and she was of course familiar with anarchist thought, the claims of which were well-known in Sydney and Melbourne at this time. She complains that most people lack the ability to live where they please and grow their own food, to be free from paying rent, and to escape tyrannical laws; this can also be seen as an anarchist perspective, and achievement of these goals is what she and other fellow-activists aim to achieve when they move to Paraguay. Also compatible with such a framework is the support that she voices here for the naturalness of the family—"marriage is the most natural position of the sexes" ("Mrs. Rose Summerfield: 'The Gospel of Discontent'" 1892)—which revolves around her belief that people should be able to marry or have children because they want to, even if they have limited finances. The anarchist influences in the thought of Rose Summerfield, who tended to think of herself as a socialist and worked actively for the ASL, will be explored in chapter 3.

Because of the way that the capitalism is organized (or not organized), people live in substandard apartments in squalid urban environments; men cannot afford to have a family, and even if they briefly can accomplish this, there is always a substantial risk that soon that ability will dry up as the economy falters. So, men avoid marrying, but illegitimate children are born. Criticizing the "diabolical doctrines" ("Mrs. Rose Summerfield: 'The Gospel of Discontent'" 1892) of Thomas Robert Malthus, whose theories have been forced by argument, government, and economics alike upon those who surely did not wish to accept them, she asks:

> How many of you working men who possess any knowledge of the iniquitous distribution of wealth, that understand the economic conditions under which we live; that know the uncertainty of the labor market; that know how fierce is the struggle for existence, feel justified in asking a woman to share your lot; to become mother of your children? You know your earnings are not sufficient to provide for, much less to maintain a family, therefore the happiness and comfort that should be yours by right of the very nature of which you are possessed, is denied you. ("Mrs. Rose Summerfield: 'The Gospel of Discontent'" 1892)

Throughout her speech, Summerfield praises the contemporary growth of discontent and tries to anticipate what good it might achieve, with the tenor being somewhat existentialist in character, and ultimately optimistic:

> Discontent is freely spreading itself over the whole of the civilised globe, may it spread and flourish, may its seeds take deep root in healthy soil, it will lighten the almost superhuman tasks the social reforms have begun. ("Mrs. Rose Summerfield: 'The Gospel of Discontent'" 1892)

Not surprisingly, the Brisbane *Worker* commented very positively on her performance in Bourke: "She is a rattling lecturer and organiser—full of fire and energy. If she came Queenslandwards there should be a good field for such a worker." In 1927, a man called William Wood, who had moved to one of the Paraguay settlements and not returned, where he had met with Summerfield and her second husband from time to time before her death, wrote a letter to a friend back in Australia in which he still recalled Rose's skillful oratory in Bourke back in 1892 ("First a Crawl and Then a Lie" 1892; "New Australia" 1927; "The World of Labour" 1892).

WORKERS' UNION ORGANIZER

Visiting Melbourne, where she had been investigating the local labor market, and had delivered a speech called "Women Workers" at Victoria Hall on Sunday, February 12, 1893, in which she focused on the inadequacy of women's pay and the need to improve educational opportunities for women, Summerfield stayed longer than she had anticipated in order to attend the second annual conference of the General Laborers' Union of Australasia, which opened on March 2, 1893, the AWU's previous name still being used. Rose was voted admittance into the conference as an official of the union, her credential being her work as the organizer of the union's Women's Division, a post which should be viewed, the union president, James Slattery, argued to the assembled membership, as equivalent to being a formally chosen delegate from a local branch. This allowed Summerfield to present the details of her activities on behalf of the union in a long speech, details of which had been circulated in advance, and which, as Nicol (1979, 27, fn 63) notes, were also printed in the *Shearers' and General Laborers' Record.* Nicol lists the date of the issue in question as being March 5, but it was actually March 15; the monthly newsletters always bore the date of the fifteenth ("General Laborers' Union of Australasia" 1893).

In that annual union meeting speech, "Resume of My Work in Connection with the General Laborers' Union, commencing 1 August 1892," Summerfield (1893b) reports that she founded the Australian Workers' Labor Bureau in order to reach "servant girls," attempting to balance the interests of the employees with those of employers, and to persuade female workers to set up branches of the union that would represent them. She also held socials at Carrington Hall in Sydney to increase the opportunities for making such contacts and further her goal. Seventy or eighty women signed up for their work-finding services, which were lower-priced than those of competitors, but the bureau received little income from these activities, and the socials were too expensive to be continued. Also, "the wrong class of men came" to the dances, and this "did us more harm than good," while some employers refused to use the union's employment services, so the bureau strategy had to be terminated ("Australian Workers: New Labour Organisation" 1892; Cooper and Patmore 2002, 8; Nicol 1979, 27–28; Spence 1893).

In October, Rose had visited Bourke, where, as noted, the actual "Gospel of Discontent" speech described earlier in the chapter was delivered on October 3, 1892. Later, she made a brief visit to Young, NSW, to talk about "The Necessity of Organisation of Women Workers," before moving on to Gundagai, NSW, where, on Tuesday, November 8, 1892, she spoke at a meeting chaired by Arthur "Andy" Rae, who was originally from New Zealand; Rae was the MLA for the Murrumbidgee area of New South Wales (MLA standing for Member of the Legislative Assembly, the title used in the past for those elected to the lower house of the New South Wales Parliament, who today are referred to as Members of Parliament [MPs]). Rose's presentation was on "Why the Workers should be Organised and Federated" (also reported as "Why Workers should be Federated and Co-operated") in which she focused to a significant extent on "Monopoly, with its attendant curse competition written in letters of blood on the gown of 'Liberty'" ("The Workers Union of N.S.W." 1892), the Broken Hill Strike, and the need for land reform; in her inimitable style, she quoted the words of Robbie Burns ("Gundagai" 1892; "Gundagai, Friday" 1892; "The Workers Union of N.S.W." 1892). Reporting on the speech, a columnist declared:

> The ladies are beginning to make themselves heard on the questions of the day. Mrs. Rose Summerfield, a lecturess connected with the Workers' Union, spoke with unmistakable voice at Gundagai last week, and with that fiery eloquence so characteristic of her sex fiercely attacked the wrongs, the injustices, and the corruption of the age. (Lyptus 1892)

Although Summerfield was pleased that her visit elicited the attention of local journalists, she felt that her appearance in Gundagai "was not successful, beyond the advertising of our Union among some hundreds of women" (Summerfield 1893b), though "whilst sincerely deploring the fact that I have not been a financial success, I think I can safely lay claim to have been an advertising success for the A.W.U." (1893b). A union of female tailors declined her invitation to merge with the AWU. While in Gundagai on the rainy evening of November 15, 1892, Rose and other union leaders, including Arthur Rae and W. W. Head and their wives attended a "Workers' Ball" at Paine Hall, which featured 28 dances, an ASU banner, and many other decorations. A similar event in September to benefit a Workers' Library had raised almost £10 for the cause ("The Workers' Ball" 1892; "The Workers' Library Ball" 1892).

At the beginning of her Gundagai lecture, "Why the Workers should be Organised and Federated," with Head sitting alongside her on the platform, and Rae having asked the audience to listen to her patiently "on account of her sex," Summerfield once again warned that the circumstances for ordinary workers were about to take a turn for the worse:

> I know dozens, scores of men, not only men but helpless women, who are truly thankful if they can manage to get one meal a day, and yet they call this "Sunny New South Wales, the paradise of the working man." Nay, friends, it is fast being turned into the hell of the working man and woman too. ("The Workers Union of N.S.W." 1892)

The housing situation at present displayed the contradictory achievements of a capitalist system that worked against the interests of most of the persons upon whom it relied for its labor, with "houses going to ruin in the suburbs of Melbourne because the people have not the means to live away from the immediate vicinity of their work, hundreds of houses idle everywhere, families living in rooms" ("The Workers Union of N.S.W." 1892).

Summerfield emphasizes the extra limits that employment imposes on most laborers, in addition to the necessity to locate oneself somewhere from which it is possible to get to the workplace on time, which may restrict the type or location of housing during the hours in which the employee is not being paid; in a Marxian sense, perhaps, she is pointing out that limitations caused by the alienation of one's labor during work hours overflow into the space where a person considers him or herself free and to have resumed their own life, which they again control. Most workers, she says, are unable to negotiate the rate of pay they receive for their job, or to take time off on the specific days when they need or desire it. At work, employees are bound to obey all instructions and can be fired if they refuse, while serious illness carries a risk of not being able to return to employment. For domestic workers, conditions are potentially even more arbitrary, as restrictions on personal liberty may last throughout the entire 24-hour day:

> [V]ery few servants in the cities can go out, when their work is finished for the day, they can sit in the kitchen cheerless and alone and not protest against it simply because the mistress has more power than they—do you not see then the necessity for organisation amongst the workers? ("The Workers Union of N.S.W." 1892)

For household employees, then, the alienation also never comes to a stop as the workplace never even recedes from view, and in Marx's terms, their ruination is complete:

> The worker puts his life into the object, and his life then belongs no longer to himself but to the object. The greater his activity, therefore, the less he possesses. What is embodied in the product of his labor is no longer his own. The greater this product is, therefore, the more he is diminished. (Marx [1844] 1932, 29; Avineri 1968, 103)

The lack of unity between employees, Summerfield continues, undermines the ability of the majority of them to obtain adequate pay, not only because many people are not members of a union, but because the division of those who are unionized into separate organizations constitutes a further barrier to improving the standard of living. Here, she advocates the merger of many groups into a very large labor organization, specifically the one for whom she is working:

> True you had unions shearers, seamen, tradesmen, mechanics, all have their separate unions, but has it never struck you workers that your education has

> been terribly neglected, that you have been and, unfortunately, many of you still are horribly conservative; you have been content with living in the moon, as it were. ("The Workers Union of N.S.W." 1892)

When employees are stronger and better organized, Rose points out, the potential for exploitation is lessened, and labor conditions can be much more controlled by the people who produce the goods and services, as the situation among some professional staffs displays:

> The solicitors, the lawyers, who do such a vast amount in the way of law, quoting and writing such a hideous mass of purely unnecessary phrases absolutely unintelligible to any ordinary mind, have they not a clique of their own, certain prices for writing a letter, a certain price demanded for obtaining justice for you, or in many cases for bungling your affairs, for very frequently converting the money of their clients to their own pockets, and lots of other little things too numerous to mention. . . . The doctors also, do they not obtain a stated price for coming to see the sick, they feel a patient's pulse, look at his tongue, write out a prescription in a language unknown to most of us and charge half a guinea, or a whole guinea; every doctor . . . does this simply because the price is strictly understood by the great bodies of physicians to be a correct one. In the same way if you want plans drawn for a house an architect will do it for a stated sum approved of by the association of architects. ("The Workers Union of N.S.W." 1892)

Here, Summerfield amusingly interprets the services of lawyers and doctors in a way that not only shows how they have gained much greater control over the work that they do, but also indicates how ordinary Australians can be taken advantage of by those less limited by the supervision of owners, shareholders, boards, or managers, as the need to cater to the patient or customer in legal or curative difficulty now begins to compete with the rather more self-serving motives of the person to whom he or she turns to for assistance. Critics of labor unions aware of the potential for such maladjustment to occur may speak of factories where the union is strong but little work is done. In the case of the initial "New Australia" colony in Paraguay, and the selfish behavior of some of the settlers on the first voyage on the *Royal Tar*, which took them to South America, even while they were still on the ship, it has been suggested by a number of commentators that the mutual aid and cooperative community-building viewed supportively by Rose, Rae, Head, and their colleagues, is much more difficult to actually achieve than they ever anticipated, because people often use any power they have gained from association with others to protect their own interests, which is at least partly the explanation for the failure of the whole New Australia experiment.

Summerfield was clearly not unaware of such potential for failure. In her Gundagai speech, she advocates "what the workers all over the world have been dreadfully slow in recognising—that is the brotherhood of man, the sisterhood of women" ("The Workers Union of N.S.W." 1892), but she identifies also the presence of "such class barriers . . . that the task of enlightenment is necessarily a very slow and tedious process" (1892). Nonetheless, having a system built on reverence for the liberty of the capitalist and the wealthy landowner who fences in a large area of nature making it inaccessible to most Australians, an economy built on low wages, is to neglect the losers in that system, the "healthy, honest able-bodied men, and comely women, and pretty children" (1892). Rather, she endorses the virtues of sisterhood and brotherhood. In her poem, "Love of Comrades," the affection that Rose expresses for her fellow workers seems even to replace the Christian love of which she was generally skeptical:

> Love of comrades, sisters, brothers,
> Love of yon for me and mine
> Neither time nor distance smothers;
> All that's best of mine and thine
> In each self blends all the others:
> Love of comrades, love divine. (Summerfield 1898g)

In another poem, "Not True" (Summerfield 1898i), Rose continues to challenge her fellow workers to cooperate as they strive to grasp what they have hitherto been denied:

> No, no! don't you believe 'tis true
> That God made man to slave and weep:
> Just stick together, dare and do,
> And be not like dumb, driven sheep.
> As life for others holds much joy,
> Up, man, and claim your lawful share!
> Your brains, your strength and worth employ;
> For labor's wrongs need swift repair. (Summerfield 1898i)

Business owners, on the other hand, she continues in her "Why the Workers Should be Organised and Federated" discourse, "are like the vampire, will not leave off until all the blood is drained from the labourer, then when disabled, helpless, get another to take his place, and so it goes on. You first have to remember that in Sydney alone there are thousands of men unemployed, so the capitalists, the exploiters, can reap their golden harvest" ("The Workers Union of N.S.W." 1892). Problems related to gold and its mining, including its role as a symbol of wealth, were often addressed by Rose Summerfield, and in this speech, once again she emphasizes the unfairness of capitalist production that involves mining:

> Who own the goldmines of New South Wales? Who are the proprietors of the vast coalmines? Come, answer me! Are the workers?—the men who court broken limbs, disease, suffering, accidents. Are these, I ask, the proprietors? You cannot tell me yes; they are not, they are not even allowed to work them except at a master's order; the men who go into these mines to find the beautiful gold which will not benefit them, to hew the shining coal which will not warm them, are the mere machines, the wage-slaves of the monopolists whose hands are ever lifted to destroy. ("The Workers Union of N.S.W." 1892)

In a letter to the *Gundagai Times* at the height of the Broken Hill miners' strike, Rose advocated the cooperative organization of work, particularly in the context of the gold mining industry planned for the Gundagai area following the discovery of the precious metal there. Such "working together as mates"—the mateship that later inspired people such as herself to emigrate to the settlements in Paraguay—would, she argued, benefit all parties involved as employees would work harder in return for a greater and more equitable share of the profits (Summerfield 1892a).

Coming originally from a gold-mining area of Victoria, Rose viewed the nature of and search for gold both symbolically and literally as an agent of the enslavement of many poorer Australians. The metal caused additional negative effects indirectly, because the pursuit of mining and the setting aside of land for its production lessened the ability of the poor in cities such as Sydney to have decent housing. In an article called "A Sermon in Stones," she argued that the desire to wear gold created the toil of miners that resulted in a range of physical ailments encountered by people who were themselves so low-paid that they would seldom encounter the metal whose very pursuit had damaged their bodies, imposing on them a cruel way of life. In a poem with the title "True Womanhood," she asks:

> If diamonds do glisten on the lily neck
> Does that add beauty to the heart that beats below?
> If gold and rubies do the nut-brown hair bedeck
> Are they a semblance of the worth of wisdom's flow? (Summerfield 1898r)

Here, Rose is as ever very much aware of the class-based effects, in this case of people's love for gold and other forms of adornment, and she argues that women are more affected by its lure than men, with damaging social consequences (Summerfield 1892a, 1896a, 1898r; "The Workers Union of N.S.W." 1892):

> Why should some mothers give forth the fruit of their love to delve in foul air; to work in water knee deep; to get crushed 'neath tons of earth because other women want gewgaws for their persons? Why do tender-hearted women, who would not crush a worm, doom their brothers to such slavish toil and unnecessary suffering in order to gratify their vanity? (Summerfield 1896a)

In response, she suggests that those who avail themselves of luxuries should be willing to compensate the full cost:

> Gold ornamentation, gold currency is not only a luxury, a superfluity, but an incentive to crime and plunder. Those who want it should be prepared to pay the proper price; that would mean insurance against accident and disease for those who work in mines; a suitable and honourable provision for all dependent on them in case of misfortune; shorter hours of labour. (Summerfield 1896a)

In this discussion of the problems caused by the pursuit of opulence, Summerfield prioritizes what she thinks would be superior goals, the basic human needs that should be satisfied before people engage in more frivolous pursuits. Maintaining the health and nutrition of one's family, and being able to spend time with friends, she suggests, are more important than securing expensive decorative items to wear (Summerfield 1896a).

In the middle of December 1892, Summerfield and Rae visited Cooma, NSW, a country town in the Snowy Mountains area to the southwest of Sydney, where Rose spoke at the School of Arts about "The Benefits of Unionism for Women Workers," advocating and then succeeding in setting up a branch of the AWU. From the point of view of the press, however, the most significant event at the area meetings was Rae's announcement on the night of Saturday, December 17, that, as the Sydney *Daily Telegraph* reported it, "All persons not unionists should be compelled to join the unions by means of a boycott. Every unionist had the right to boycott every non-unionist and starve him into joining" ("Labor Meeting at Cooma" 1892). Possibly Rae's statement and the reaction to it will have undermined Summerfield's (1893b) confidence in her report "that if the work of organising is carried out in a proper manner . . . the women in the country towns will soon be brought to see the advantage of unionism" ("General Gleanings" 1892; "Labor Meeting at Cooma" 1892; "Mr. Rae, M.P., on Boycotting" 1892; "New South Wales" 1892; "New South Wales Mems" 1892; "Sydney" 1892).

Following the demise of the Labor Bureau, Summerfield visited private employment offices in Sydney and Melbourne, posing as a job applicant, to obtain information about the state of the market from the perspective of employees (Spence 1893; Summerfield 1893b). Reflecting upon this experience, and the fact the bureau was misunderstood by some of those who encountered the innovation as mainly a service to benefit employers, she concluded: "The system showed me pretty plainly how it was that our office had to close at a loss" (Summerfield 1893b).

In her report, Rose also criticized what she thought was a negative aspect of women working outside their homes for low pay:

> I have found through association with various workers that women's cheap labor in many instances forces men out of employment, and causes incalculable mischief in the community. The sweating system is carried on chiefly through its medium, and the women who take work home at a cheap rate are the great cause of wages in factories and workshops being reduced. (Summerfield 1893b)

Elsewhere, in a letter published under her "Sisters' Column" in the *Hummer*, Rose attempted to address the fact that having very low prices for clothing does not allow the seamstresses who toil making it to receive a living wage; more than a hundred years later, this problem continues to exist on a global basis, contributing to women's second-class status as they labor. It is clear from the retail market in Melbourne in early 1893 that, for many, poverty was getting worse. This situation, Rose writes, "indeed is one of the truest signs of the times, for women dearly love bargains" and presumably would be buying clothes in greater quantity if it were at all possible. Perhaps, she continues, alluding to the fierce spirit demonstrated by women in ancient Sparta, their contemporaries should be more willing to haggle for higher tailoring pay than only to negotiate a bargain in a store. Moreover, women's tendency to passively accept their disadvantage in the workplace is unnecessary and damaging, and failure to see the benefits of standing up for yourself is to miss the point that the quality of family life would be improved if they did: "Men would love and admire strong, brave, earnest women who had enough soul in them to enable them to rise above their wretched surroundings" (Summerfield 1893c).

The letter, which was published a month later, is dated February 28, 1893, and the theme of women loving a deal appears also in a slightly earlier and longer piece that can be found in the *Shearers' and General Laborers' Record* issue of February 15, 1893. Summerfield's name is absent from this article, but the writing style and the topics covered in it make it very likely that she was the author. Then, the next month, the *Shearers' and General Laborers' Record* contained her detailed report of her activities working with the General Laborers' Union, which did bear her name. In the earlier piece, Rose writes:

> Woman's passion for a bargain has become a proverb and a source of much satire, though it may be doubted whether in some cases the purchaser really knows the absolute cost of her bargain. . . . No article of dress is more popular

> at present than a cheap blouse, and of these the cheapest and most inferior kind sell as low as 1s. 3d. apiece. The best worker, with the fastest appliances cannot make more than seven in a day, which at 2½d. apiece, the price at which an outcry is being raised, gives the experienced mantle-maker 1s. 5½d. for her day's work. The great majority of the workers, however, cannot make seven blouses, and their earnings are reduced accordingly. Those who know the cost of living in Melbourne, with almost everything taxed, will be able to estimate what chance these girls have in the struggle for a decent existence. ("Women's Work and Pay: Starvation Wages" 1893) [Under the pre-decimal system of currency used at the time, there were twelve pennies (denoted by d.) in a shilling (denoted by s.) and twenty shillings in a pound (denoted by £).]

This article also contains some of Summerfield's interviews with such mantle-makers (cloakmakers) and other seamstresses who reported that piece rates were often changed in a downward direction, further depressing wages, while tardiness resulted in inappropriate fines; the numbers of people employed in tailoring of this sort varied considerably, from time to time throwing some out of work. Without a union, they could only accept the loss of income or quit, and perhaps, as one supervisor advised when employees challenged a new lower rate paid per blouse, "get a man to keep you like other girls"—a comment reflecting the sad state of gender relations. Two mantle-makers who had arrived recently from Scotland, where they had done the same type of work, and were now encountering some of these problems in Melbourne, said that they hoped to return home when they could ("Women's Work and Pay: Starvation Wages" 1893). Pointing out that most of the people victimized by their employment in the clothing industry are women, Rose elsewhere reminds the reader that they also have another role in society to play:

> Wages paid to dressmakers and girls in laundries are very poor; how they manage to live, especially those who have no settled homes with parents, is a puzzle—it is truly a case of the immorality of the production for profit system that so besmirches our civilization. How much more glaring is the evil when one considers that these are to be the mothers of our race. What a world of pathos in the thought! (Summerfield 1898q)

Summerfield (1898p) also expressed skepticism about the role of quasi-charitable institutions that provided relief to the disadvantaged and employed them in return for the assistance, without allowing them any additional payment. In Sydney, such charities were involved in making underwear, for instance, which meant that the clothing they produced was available very cheaply, which had the effect of lowering the wages of other seamstresses who worked elsewhere. Places of refuge such as the One Sydney Rescue

Society, she notes, spent significant amounts of revenue on their administrators' salaries, rather than on the welfare of their charges:

> [A] few smug, canting hypocrites get good salaries and positions, and very often good homes into the bargain, through the woes of the most abject, indigent poor of this fair land. (Summerfield 1898p)

At the end of June 1893, in response to a request from the New Lambton, NSW branch of the ASL that she visit that area and speak locally, Rose Summerfield gave a series of four lectures, starting with a delivery about "Socialism" at the Mechanics' Institute in Plattsburg on the afternoon of Sunday, June 25, and continuing the same evening at the Hall of Science in Newcastle. At night on June 26, she talked about "The Wrongs and Rights of Labour" at Lathlean's Hall in New Lambton. Pointing out interconnections between the membership of the N.S.W. Senate, to which, in her earlier speech in Gundagai she had referred to as "that huge blubbering mass of inconsistency and misrepresentation, the Upper House" ("The Workers Union of N.S.W." 1892), and what she saw as the goal of large-scale owners and banks to crush ordinary working people, she next turned to another of her familiar topics, the land monopoly that made it close to impossible for ordinary people to purchase homes in rural areas, confining them to squalid conditions in urban environments, where the presence of and competition from "the Mongolian race" (i.e., Chinese immigrants) undermined their ability to attain a fair price for their labor ("Lecture at New Lambton" 1893; "Smoke Ho!" 1893a). A Newcastle area newspaper covered her third speech, and noted as follows the outline of another of Rose's major concerns:

> In conclusion the speaker called on all women to come from their seclusion, and assist in the work of propagating the principals [*sic*] of socialism. ("Lecture at New Lambton" 1893)

Notices promoting the visit indicated that "Ladies" were "especially invited," as Summerfield in tandem pursued the goals of socialism and women's improvement. The fourth performance, initially announced as being scheduled for the Mechanics' Institute in Merewether, actually took place in that town at the Albert Victor Hall ("Lectures: Socialism" 1893; "Merewether: Lecture" 1893; "Plattsburg" 1893). In 1895, Summerfield returned to the Plattsburg venue, on August 18 of that year delivering a talk on a different topic, "The Enigmas of Life," which the local socialists hoped would initiate support for a regular Sunday series of such talks ("Current News" 1895).

For Summerfield, and for many of her AWU and ASL colleagues, the British unionist Ben Tillett was a role model, a pioneer of the New Unionism, and his visit to Australia and New Zealand in 1897–1898 allowed many of them to meet with him and to listen to him speak. As the general secretary of the Tea Operatives' and General Labourers' Association (TOGLA), his activities on behalf of dock workers in London, a campaign that, at the prompting of Rose's fellow-activist Gilbert S. Casey, was partially financed by unions in Australia, had in 1889 resulted in a successful citywide work stoppage that resulted in an increase in the longshoremen's pay, an event that is now widely known as the London Dock Strike. Later in life, Tillett's continued activism would lead, in 1922, to the integration of many smaller unions into the Transport and General Workers' Union (TGWU), an effort that in many ways mirrored the activities of Summerfield, Spence, and other leaders who created the AWU. After a number of unsuccessful attempts to win election, Tillett served in the British House of Commons, and became the chairperson of the Trades Union Congress (TUC) ("Ben Tillett" 1898; "Notes and Comments" 1897; "Section—The Great 1889 Dockers' Strike" 2001; Summerfield 1897).

Not surprisingly, the piece that Rose wrote in the Brisbane *Worker* (Summerfield 1897) about Ben Tillett at a time when he was sick is very flattering, and she emphasizes the sincerity of his commitment to women's rights. "Far be it from me to assume the role of prophet," she wrote, "but this much can be said with absolute certainty: Ben Tillet's visit to Australia will have a lasting, beneficial effect upon the Reform movement generally" (Summerfield 1897). However, for Verity Burgmann (1985a), Australian radicals' admiration for foreign socialist leaders like Tillett was excessive and an example of what she refers to as "a cultural cringe, a tendency to hero-worship leading British and American, and to some extent, continental European, socialists":

> In Sydney, the Australian Socialist League was overwhelmed by the magnificence of Ben Tillett. The League's paper at the time, the *Northern People*, considered that his features were 'those of a man of high intellectual powers', that he had 'the heart of a lion' and that it was his 'human magnetism' that swayed the audience at the Trades Hall. Rose Summerfield, who interviewed the convalescent Tillett for the *Northern People*, was clearly bowled over by the man. According to her, on the sickbed lay a man of the most striking personality it had ever been her good fortune to meet. (Burgmann 1985a, 7–8)

Moreover, while in response to Burgmann, Daphne Gollan (1986, 98) defends the attitude of Summerfield and her allies, because "[i]n their innocence they thought of themselves as internationalists" (98), she also specifically condemns Rose's coverage as follows:

> As for Rose Summerfield's pen portrait of Tillett, that is familiar nineteenth century literary gush. (Gollan 1986, 98)

Admittedly, the parts of Rose's episodic and quixotic account in the Brisbane *Worker* portraying Tillett as a "super-sensitive" boy running away from home at the age of seven, winning a bet in a Russian port by tweaking a guard's nose, and taking care of an unwanted child who would eventually succumb to tuberculosis are syrupy stuff. The tale of how "her wee lad, smarting with a sense of the great injustice done his mother fled from his home" (Summerfield 1897) may strike some who read it as somewhat counterproductive, especially considering that Tillett was a man of many significant accomplishments, and Summerfield was a highly literate, knowledgeable writer whose command of persuasive oratory was instantly apparent (1897).

Some of Tillett's views were not typical of other union activists and, in particular, his opposition to Jewish immigration to the U.K. and to the existing presence of Jewish immigrants, whom he characterized as members of an alien culture and as the enemy of ordinary workers, has understandably been criticized. During his visits to Australian towns and cities, local mayors were asked to chair meetings at which Tillett spoke, a practice regarded as a role quite customary to their office, but some mayors including the ones in Melbourne, Ballarat, and Broken Hill declined to do this, since they disagreed with his opinions, though not necessarily because of his anti-Semitism ("Ben Tillett" 1898; "Ben Tillett and Melbourne's Mayor" 1898; "Ben Tillett and the Mayor of Melbourne" 1898; Maley 1897; Virdee 2017, 361, 368). Rose's views about the wisdom of allowing "Australian" workers to be undermined in the workplace and elsewhere by immigrants from Asia, Southern Europe, and New Caledonia has similarly been criticized, and its significance and extent can be debated, as indicated in chapter 4.

Chapter 2

Campaigner for Women's Rights

NEW WOMAN

Rose Summerfield was actively involved in campaigning for women's suffrage, and wanted to change the nature of the marriage contract to improve the status and mental health of women, and she was familiar with the stance of the "New Woman" perspective that was taking place contemporaneously in the light of interest in Henrik Ibsen's 1879 play, *A Doll's House*, and from its other formulations, such as the character of "Miss Daisy Miller" in Henry James's short novel, *Daisy Miller* (1878), who says "I have never allowed a gentleman to dictate to me, or to interfere with anything I do" (James [1878] 1966, 34), and about whom a potential suitor comments, "It was impossible to regard her as a perfectly well-conducted young lady; she was wanting in a certain indispensable delicacy" (35). In the United States, *A Doll's House* and its heroine, Nora, would at the beginning of the twentieth century attract the attention of Margaret Sanger and Emma Goldman, and in Japan, the Bluestocking Society (*Seitō-sha*), who would found their new feminist journal, *Seitō*, in 1911, the year that Ibsen's play was first staged in Japan, took such an interest in the play, later publishing a translation of it in *Seitō*, that they were soon being referred to as the "Japanese Noras" (Reich and Fukuda 1976, 284; Shone 2019, 200–201, 246). In Australia, the play was first performed in Melbourne on Sunday, September 15, 1889 (Hoare 2006; "Princess's Theatre—A Doll's House" 1889a). The theater critic of the Melbourne *Argus* who attended that performance at the city's Princess's Theatre found the play excessively "didactic," complaining "that the character of Nora in the third act is unnatural, and repels rather than invites sympathy; while the lesson which the dramatist wishes to convey is neither a wholesome, nor an elevated or elevating one" ("Princess's Theatre: 'A Doll's House'" 1889b).

At a meeting on Sunday, February 17, 1895, at Leigh House in Castlereagh Street in Sydney, a dance hall until its demise in 1929, where many radicals met over the years in upstairs meeting rooms, Summerfield, who was possibly aware of the *Argus* correspondent's criticism, or at least familiar with comments of a similar nature, defended the concept of the New Woman and of its advocate, Ibsen, against what she termed "the contempt and sneers of ill-paid journalists" ("About the New Woman" 1895) who were attempting to demean this widespread emancipatory movement. Bearing witness to Rose's accuracy on that point, and doing so with a certain amount of cynical amusement, the Sydney *Daily Telegraph* reporter of this event noted in his account that "[t]here were several young ladies in the audience. Either they were curious spectators or they hadn't found sweethearts yet. It is only when a woman gets near the other side of 30 that she begins to have 'views' on the marriage question" ("About the New Woman" 1895). In truth, Rose continued, the New Woman wished to improve the nature of women's experience, and to raise children in a more sophisticated environment. Marriage, she argued, could be customized to the needs and interests of the couple in question, need not be standardized at all, and should not be sanctified with false reference to religious authority ("About the New Woman" 1895; "Brevities" 1895; O'Sullivan 1929):

> "The god which joins most people together," said Mrs. Summerfield, "is the god of Mammon, the spirit of selfishness, and the dominion of lust. That is the rule upon which marriage is contracted nowadays." ("About the New Woman" 1895)

Another reporter, conceding that "I do not agree with Mrs. Summerfield that woman is mentally and physically equal to man—as yet" (Faustine 1895), presented Rose's lecture as being scientifically inaccurate and also as an instance of inappropriate women's rights shrieking designed to offend husbands:

> One regrets that Mrs. Summerfield, in her address on the "New Woman" question, should have adopted, in one or two particulars, that tone from which those who recognise that what affects the woman affects the man equally pray to be delivered. (Faustine 1895)

Rose was not the only member of her social circle attracted to the New Woman perspective. Around the time when she was scheduling her "The Gospel of Discontent" speech with the Australian Socialist League (ASL) executive committee three years earlier, an associate, Mrs. J. R. Ashton, was setting up another lecture designed to promote socialism, titled "Ibsen's Heroines" ("Australian Socialist League" 1892b). It may come as a surprise to the reader to hear that the critic, "Faustine," was in fact the pen name of the same Mrs. J. R. Ashton, who often, as was the practice back then, identified herself using the initials of her husband, the artist, J. R. Ashton. Her own name, following her marriage, was Eliza Ann Ashton. At the time of her death, a *Daily Telegraph* reporter commented that "[i]f dissecting Ibsen, . . . she was . . .

sure of a tribute to her deep knowledge of dramatists" ("Death of Mrs. J. R. Ashton: A Well-Known Lady Writer" 1900). However, as "Faustine," at least, unlike Summerfield, she was apparently not an admirer of Ibsen, nor that of Rose ("Death of Mrs. J. R. Ashton: A Well-Known Lady Writer" 1900; "Mrs. Ashton Again" 1892; "Woman and the Marriage Laws" 1892).

Walking around the streets of Sydney, Rose ponders "the women with little children, hungry and ragged, clinging to their skirts" (Summerfield 1895b) as poverty becomes worse, and mothers, unable to find a legitimate job, are forced to sell their bodies to feed their families. Will people like herself, New Women of charm and greater affluence, eventually experience the same fate?

> Will the new women be like them? Will their spawn breed aught but blots like themselves? Will the women who think on the social problems of the curses of monopoly ever give themselves up to this holocaust that festers and rots and thrives[?] (Summerfield 1895b)

In the red light area, prostitutes openly flaunt their wares but, Summerfield suggests, many of the same factors are at work on adjacent streets in the dance halls and other places where attractively dressed women drink wine, seeking pleasure and the attention of men:

> The sight of a shapely bust and naked shoulders, upon which men cast strange glances, made me doubt the purity; for in that other street I saw the same—there it was indecent; but here, of course, we were in a fashionable crowd. (Summerfield 1895b)

Unfortunately, this less obvious form of prostitution and women's degradation has become socially acceptable, a development that does not augur positively for succeeding generations:

> [O]ur fine ladies will expose their natural charms in ball-room and theatre, so that the highest bidder can be tempted. (Summerfield 1895b)

Like Mary Wollstonecraft, Louise Michel, Victoria C. Woodhull, Emma Goldman, and other feminist thinkers, Summerfield in this way identified conventional marriage as a form of prostitution. Rose dismissed established justifications such as an apparent need to produce children, along with the pressures that derive from lustful urges and other varieties of selfishness, or from the commercialization of family life, advocating instead an openness to and acceptance of different approaches to what an emancipatory form of marriage might mean. Understandably concerning her own freethinking perspective, she mocked "the cant of religious ceremonies," considering them inappropriate modes of dedication for a future age that would be founded on reason ("About the New Woman" 1895). Nonetheless, she considered reason itself to have limited application in areas where despondency undermined many people's ability to cope, and she believed the disadvantaged needed to be viewed with sympathy:

> Reason the few, the strong may charm;
> Love shields the weak, the frail from harm;
> Though Intellect the proud may sway,
> 'Tis Love divine makes glad our day. (Summerfield 1899a)

Summerfield often describes in terms of class difference the way that life in the modern city has undermined the possibilities for both women and men to enjoy their existence.

> And, Workman, specially digest this: Your own class have your identical interests at heart, they rise or fall with you, they are victims of the same despotism, coerced through their stomachs the same as you, therefore trust them, combine with them, share with them the arduous labor of enlightening the masses to their true worth, to the life of comparative plenty they could enjoy did they but awaken to the fact that at present they are occupying far worse positions than the negro slaves of America in the sixties, and that this position is forced upon them through upholders of a base system of profit-mongering. (Summerfield 1898s)

For example, she empathizes with the women who work in stores, feigning interest in fashions that more affluent shoppers are thinking about purchasing, but tired from their toil, miserable, bored with their jobs that offer no opportunity for advancement, maybe nursing an aching back (Summerfield 1895a):

> "A beautiful glove, indeed." "I can recommend this make." Mere parrot utterances. These fret me much. Many of these pallid women will some day clasp babies to their breasts, and when we read of infants' deaths we scarcely marvel—we who have watched the goings and comings of a big city—for we feel the sap is gone from flowers that grow in arid places, so know their buds are sapless too. (Summerfield 1895a)

THE TWO ROSES

Although Rose Summerfield would become the president of the Waverley, NSW branch of the Womanhood Suffrage League (WSL), she became engaged in an argument with Rose Scott, one of the founders of the League, and specifically with Mrs. M. English (whose complete first name is now unknown), who would later become the president of the organization's Summer Hill, NSW branch, that raised a number of issues about what feminists might and might not want (Hearn 2004, 76; Nicol 1979, 27). In her column in the *Hummer*, the Wagga, NSW weekly newspaper that would the next month change its name to the *Worker*, Summerfield took exception to the content of a speech that English had made in which she argued that women should be able to take any type of work, including occupations in the construction industry. For Summerfield, it was not difficult to satirize that argument, pointing out that women climbing ladders in short skirts would not enjoy such employment or feel that it contributed to their dignity. "Surely," she objected, "in this young country, with its democratic ideas, and the fair amount of freedom bestowed on women, we do not want to degrade our womankind thus" (Summerfield 1892d). Although Rose Summerfield claimed that such a situation had actually occurred in Poland in the past, it seems unlikely that tolerating embarrassment such as this would have been obligatory if the range of occupations available to women were increased. Similarly, she makes a somewhat questionable argument that shoemaking is also an unsuitable "unwomanly" profession due to the heaviness of the leather and the nature of machinery and nails, standing up all day, and coming into contact with grime, although she also points out much more significant issues relating to the way that men might treat female colleagues and the need for women to be paid at the same rate as men. The situation may change in the future, but at present, Summerfield suggests, the demands on women to bear children and to maintain their complexions, physique, and ladylike demeanor would make such expansions of the labor market inappropriate. But for the present, she sees "Mrs English and her fellow women suffragists" as attempting "to force worse ills upon that portion of the community they evidently know so little about" (Summerfield 1892d). In her Gundagai lecture, "Why the Workers should be Organised and Federated," she also pursued her claim, but on that occasion criticizing government economic policies that she believed had "damning results that sent our young girls into factories and mills to compete with the men, that keeps the same maidens ragged and cheerless and well-nigh homeless" ("The Workers Union of N.S.W." 1892). She continued:

> In England, at the present time, there are over 6000 women in the coalmines in order to help their husbands eke out a scanty existence; this is a monstrous, most cruel state of things, and should not be allowed to exist for many reasons. In the first place it is thoroughly unsuitable employment for a woman, it makes them rough and coarse, and it is horrible to think of a woman who will become a mother, a rearer of children, working, at toil that is bad enough even for strong men. ("The Workers Union of N.S.W." 1892)

Responding to Summerfield's attack, Rose Scott pointed out that the organization was open to many different viewpoints, including those of English. Scott also complained that, in the hands of Summerfield's article, the opinions of English had been attributed to the League as a whole, a claim that did not necessarily pertain. Encouraging Summerfield to come to the League's gatherings, she pointed out: "At our meetings we do not wish to check liberty of speech. All views are interesting, even though we may not agree with them" (Scott 1892c).

An earlier Sydney *Evening News* report on a speech that Mrs. English gave to a NSW-wide meeting of the Womanhood Suffrage League on March 9, 1892, presents her beliefs somewhat differently. On that occasion, English objected to the fact that men were often given easier, lighter tasks, while many women were degraded by what they had to do to make money. Instead, according to the article, she advocated "a system under which the light work in every branch and industry would be apportioned to the women and the heavier to the men" ("Womanhood Suffrage League" 1892). If the paper's narrative were accurate, it would mean that English was at another time arguing a somewhat opposite position to the one she was accused of promoting by Summerfield and which was then defended by Scott.

Responding to Scott in a column titled "The War of the Roses," Summerfield argued that since English occupied a prominent place within her organization, it was reasonable to suppose that she spoke for the majority when communicating her "extreme views" (Summerfield 1892i), opinions in favor of allowing women to do any type of labor whatsoever, which other suffragists had also from time to time been heard advocating as well. Later in the year, English wrote to the Sydney Trades and Labour Council, an organization with which a number of unions were affiliated, offering to help organize dressmakers and hatmakers, but her assistance was rejected because the Council felt her knowledge of the industry was insufficient (Nicol 1979, 27).

On April 2, 1893, Summerfield gave a presentation at Leigh House on "Women Workers." Focusing on those engaged in the manufacture of clothing and the poor conditions they encountered at work, she called for imposition of a new Factory Act that would improve regulation of this industry. Rose Scott, who attended the meeting, asked Summerfield for a copy of the existing regulations, saying she could use the document to facilitate work with a member of parliament. Summerfield promised Scott she would come to a WSL meeting, and she soon became active in the group and, in less than a year, the president of its new Waverley branch; on June 14, 1893, she was elected to its statewide governing council, and by November of that year, she was presenting herself as one of the members (Hearn 2004, 76–77; "News of the Week" 1893; Nicol 1979, 27; "St. Mary's Cathedral" 1893; Summerfield 1892i, 1893a; "Womanhood Suffrage League" 1893a, 1893b).

She now defended the League's activities, including its desire to give the vote to women as follows:

> We are not a body of women meeting together for amusement, but banded together to add our voice and work to that of the foremost guard of politicians who are prepared to treat females as rational human beings. (Summerfield 1893a)

Nonetheless, in a letter she wrote to the *Sydney Morning Herald*, which was published in the paper on November 24, 1893, she took pains to point out that her own remarks should not be taken as necessarily representing those of the WSL organization (Summerfield 1893d).

WOMAN SUFFRAGE

At a meeting held on August 9, 1893, the NSW-wide Womanhood Suffrage League voted to allow the formation of local branches, which it was felt would facilitate the expansion of its agenda. A committee was formed to draft a new constitution; among its members were Rose Summerfield and Rose Scott ("The Womanhood Suffrage League" 1893; "Womanhood Suffrage League" 1893c). Branches were then quite quickly formed, in Alexandria, Auburn, Granville, Paddington, Petersham, Randwick, Rylstone, and Waverley. Typically, the first resolution considered in the process of setting up a local affiliate would be similar to that passed by the Paddington branch: "That it is equitable and expedient that the franchise be accorded to women on the same basis as to men" ("Womanhood Suffrage" 1894a, 1894b, 1894c; "Womanhood Suffrage League" 1894b; "Women's Suffrage League" 1894).

On February 26, 1894, the League held a meeting at Petersham Town Hall that featured speeches by both of the Roses, Summerfield and Scott, and ended with a vote to create the Petersham branch; about 200 people attended. While Scott presented her familiar arguments that focused exclusively on the desirability of universal adult suffrage as a means of educating the citizenry and achieving a higher character of behavior among those who ran for office, Summerfield's critique was more wide-ranging. She questioned whether the role of women should revolve exclusively around the care of children, and emphasized the value to low-paid families of having access to a second income. She made it clear that her agenda would not be accomplished immediately just because the franchise was achieved ("Womanhood Suffrage: Meeting at Petersham" 1894):

> The right to vote was all that they were asking from the men—at present, she added significantly. They wanted the vote and wanted to take away the stain

> which rested on the legislators of this country. The women would try to alter the social system that aimed at perpetuating present wrongs. ("Womanhood Suffrage: Meeting at Petersham" 1894)

On September 6, 1894, a deputation from the WSL that included both Rose Scott and Rose Summerfield met with the NSW premier, George H. Reid, to discuss the importance of giving the vote to women, as well as a related issue, the consequences of state government contracts for the manufacture of clothing that were being fulfilled under sweatshop conditions; the premier expressed sympathy for both concerns but promised no quick remedy for either of them. The members of the WSL were aware of allied developments in other parts of the world and of writers such as Olympe de Gouges, Mary Wollstonecraft, and John Stuart Mill and their writings, and they used these examples to bolster their claims that Australian women were entitled to vote ("Womanhood Suffrage" 1894d; "Womanhood Suffrage League" 1894a; "Woman's Suffrage" 1894; "Women's Suffrage" 1894). Unfortunately, some of the impressions of the League's activities that might be gleaned from perusal of the Sydney newspapers were so unflattering that Scott ironically advised that "if ridicule were the test of truth," their members "must thank those papers which had generously supplied them with it for giving them the opportunity of showing that the female mind was not so powerless to withstand the shafts of ridicule as was generally supposed" ("Womanhood Suffrage League" 1893a). An earlier meeting, this time with Reid's predecessor, Sir George Dibbs, had resulted in a promise to communicate the ladies' arguments in favor of suffrage to his Cabinet, but it seemed there had been no further action taken on that promise, a denouement that Scott indicated now emphasized further the need for women to be able to vote. A subsequent meeting between the WSL and Reid on March 14, 1895, that included Scott and Summerfield, was similarly unsuccessful ("Womanhood Suffrage League" 1893a; "Woman's Suffrage" 1895). Women would receive the right to vote in New South Wales in 1902.

In January 1894, the Waverley (a suburb to the east of Sydney) branch of the Womanhood Suffrage League had been formed. By May, its membership had grown to 65, and the desire to extend the franchise came to occupy a number of its meetings as well as the activities of its president, Rose Summerfield, although the latter retained some of her skepticism that voting would be the most important goal for women to achieve, a position that set up, at least on a philosophical level, a second battle between the two Roses. Nonetheless, at the first public meeting of the branch, members indicated the desirability of obtaining the support of men presently representing the area, while Summerfield discoursed on the significance of the votes for women issue. In gatherings at Lovett's Hall on Spring Street in Waverley, Summerfield, who was now no longer organizing for the GLU/AWU, took the opportunity to discuss some of her other priorities and themes such as the New Woman and the need to improve the character of marriage. One meeting featured a debate about another of her interests, the role of religion, and its effects on the campaign for women's right to vote ("The Art Society" 1894; "Let the Women Be Heard" 1894; "Waverley Womanhood Suffrage League" 1895b; "Waverley Woman's Suffrage League" 1895; "Womanhood Suffrage" 1894a; "Womanhood Suffrage League" 1894a; "Woman's Suffrage: Waverley Branch Meeting" 1895). In some ways, the contrast between the two Roses resembles the differences in the United States between two allies, Susan B. Anthony, a Quaker who focused mainly on winning the vote, and Elizabeth Cady Stanton, who like Summerfield questioned the role of marriage, wanted to make it easier to obtain a divorce, sympathized with the poor, tended to view Christianity in a negative way, and expressed concerns about excessive drinking by men. But while Anthony and Cady Stanton grew further apart, Summerfield and Stone were able to cooperate closely (Shone 2019, ch. 7). After Summerfield had departed for Paraguay, Rose Scott offered her assistance to a Tailoresses' Union of NSW strike in Sydney over pay led by the future New Zealand Labour Party leader, Harry Holland, in July 1901 (Burgmann 1985a); it would have been a cause central to Summerfield's heart.

At one of the Waverley meetings, freethinker Peter McNaught spoke on "The Evolution of Democracy." He pointed out that "[u]ntil equal privileges with men were granted to women, true democracy would never be attained" ("Woman Suffrage" 1895), an argument that retains its resonance more than a century later as the right of a person to have control over her own body and thus to be able to terminate a pregnancy remains outlawed in many places around the world and under attack in many others, often on account of opposition that is based on theological dogma. The issue of religion would become problematic for the New Australia settlement in Paraguay. In a letter to the *Worker*, McNaught portrayed the havoc-wreaking struggles encountered by the Paraguay settlements as resulting to some extent from William Lane's emphasis on religion, through his endorsement of a kind of religiosity-based communism:

> If an acceptance of theological belief is necessary to membership in the [New Australia Co-operative Settlement] Association, then it ceases to be co-operative and merges into sectarianism of the worst type, plus co-operation. If I read Lane correctly, his message can mean nothing else than an attempt to make bread and butter depend on assent to a theological belief, which to me is about the worst state of society conceivable—the surest and most effective method of making hypocrites that could be devised. (McNaught 1894)

Instead, matters of religion, McNaught argued, should be left to the conscience of the individual and not forced onto others (Hannan 1966, 160; McNaught 1894; "Waverley Womanhood Suffrage League" 1895c; "Woman Suffrage" 1895).

Another Waverley evening saw Frank Fox deliver a lecture on "The Limitation of Law," while George Black, MLA, spoke about political economy and answered participants' questions. At a different meeting, a man called Professor Scott discussed "Women's Work and Wages," emphasizing the need for women to be independent and have equivalent access to education. In a presentation titled "Marvels of Ancient Peru—the Civilisation of Then and To-day," Summerfield compared the allocation of land long ago in Peru with the property laws of Australia that she saw as lying at the root of much of the poverty in the then colony. A speaker called Percy Wakefield also addressed the land issue and a number of related matters, advocating the use of referenda, saying he preferred a system of pure democracy. Another meeting featured two presentations, one on "Sophia Forovskaia," an inspirational nihilist-influenced character in Alphonse Daudet's novel, *Port Salvation*, and one promoting the desirability of women and men working together cooperatively to improve the workings of government (Dunstan 2003, 117, 333; "In the Bush" 1893; James 1986; "Lectures: Marvels of Ancient Peru" 1895; "Port Salvation" 1883; "The Labor Platform" 1894; "Waverley Womanhood Suffrage League 1894, 1895b, 1895d; "Womanhood Suffrage" 1897).

Another of the more wide-ranging issues that concerned the ladies and men of the Waverley branch, and prompted the collection of funds to achieve its remedy, was the fact that the National Art Gallery of New South Wales lacked a portrait of just one of the colony's premiers, Sir John Robertson, whose long tenure had seen him implement land reform and achieve some secularization of education. Given Rose's use of dances to attract the interest of women to her various causes, and the recitations and songs that she personally contributed to ASL and other meetings, notwithstanding her collateral concerns about the ways that some women dressed and acted at entertainment events, it is not surprising that the Waverley women held their own annual social with music, dancing, and refreshments ("Black Labor" 1892; "Brevities" 1894; "Impracticability of Socialism" 1892; "Intercolonial News: New South Wales" 1895; "Shelley's Centenary: Celebration at the School of Arts" 1892; "Sir John Robertson" 1895; "Waverley Womanhood Suffrage Social" 1895; "Woman's Suffrage: Waverley Branch Meeting" 1895). When, in May 1894, Summerfield was identified in print by a certain journalist, Eliza Ann Ashton, (who would next year criticize Rose's lecture on the New Woman), as no longer attending the Waverley meetings, the following question was prompted:

> But what has become of Mrs. Rose Summerfield, lately? Waverley is her own locality; and one wonders at the non-appearance of her name in such a goodly list of indefatigables. (Faustine 1894)

Back presiding over a meeting of the Waverley branch on January 4, 1895, that elected its officers for the coming year, Summerfield listened to a presentation by Gilbert S. Casey, the local agent of the New Australia Co-operative Settlement Association, who expressed support for involving women to a greater extent in public affairs. Following her marriage to Jack Cadogan in 1897, Rose and her husband, influenced by the attractiveness of the heavily promoted "New Australia" project, would in 1899 travel to Paraguay, where each remained until their respective deaths, initially at the Cosme settlement, despite at times encountering considerable disappointment and nursing an unfilled desire to return to Australia. In his talk to the Waverley women, more than 40 of whom were in attendance, Casey emphasized that the first batch of emigrants to the initial "New Australia" community, who had now taken up residence in Paraguay, had already attained a condition of equality between the sexes, a statement that many critics would, over the coming years, point out was in no way true. Two weeks later, on January 18, 1895, Summerfield, Casey, and McNaught were in attendance as the passenger ship SS *Hauroto*, carrying 31 new emigrants bound for the original New Australia settlement, left for Wellington, New Zealand, where they were scheduled to transfer to the SS *Rimutaka* and travel on to Montevideo. In March, the three supporters were also present to say farewell to passengers on the SS *Wakatipu*, which was similarly heading for Paraguay by way of New Zealand and Uruguay; among those traveling was Annie Lane, returning to Colonia Cosme, which had been created following disagreement between the earliest colonists, and where her husband, New Australia founder William Lane, who had caused most of the conflict, was now the chairperson ("New Australia: Arrival of the Royal Tar" 1895; "New Australia: Fresh Departure to the Settlement" 1895; "Waverley Womanhood Suffrage League" 1895a; "Womanhood Suffrage" 1895; "Woman Suffrage: Address by Mr. Casey" 1895).

As she answered Summerfield's complaint about English's views, Rose Scott took care to emphasize that the main function of the Womanhood Suffrage League, from her point of view, was to obtain the right to vote, a claim that had already attracted some considerable reflection on the part of Summerfield. Back in 1892, Summerfield had spoken in opposition to extending the right to vote to females, because she said most women were not seeking that change, which should be delayed until a majority indicated their support; she felt achieving the franchise now would distract attention from more important issues with which they enjoyed competence, such as taking care of the poor and other charity work, while some might turn their attention to becoming candidates themselves ("Woman's Rights" 1892). As revealed in newspaper coverage of her lecture titled "Problems for Woman Suffragists," which she had delivered on Sunday, June 5, 1892, in Leichhardt, on the west side of Sydney, Rose Summerfield provided a hint of the opinion she would later raise elsewhere, that there was a class-based difference in support for, or opposition to, allowing women to vote. She commented during her lecture as follows:

> "There is . . . a class of women with husbands or relatives with more money than brains, anxious to get into Parliament. Such women would not hesitate to spend their money for the relief of necessitous people in the hope of securing votes at election time. Extend the franchise to these women, and there would always be poor Joneses and Smiths, and the 'bountiful lady' would be a created necessity. ("Woman's Rights" 1892)

Much of Rose Scott's activity, however, centered on the vote question. For example, Scott argued in an article in the *Hummer* and in a speech she gave at a Unitarian church in Sydney, that allowing men to have all the responsibility for lawmaking was unfair, and that women should take more responsibility for the rules and regulations and traditions that governed them. Unfortunately, if women are not struggling with poverty, they tend to focus on their personal domestic arrangements, in their relative comfort shutting out danger, but also losing awareness of the various social problems that surround us; the franchise would thus have an educational effect, turning female attention to public affairs. If women made all the rules, she writes, it is obvious that they would make some mistakes, yet women routinely concede control of this area of human life to their husbands and fathers, failing to acknowledge the obvious, that money is often wasted by elected politicians, and legislation is seldom "honest, sober, and moral" (Scott 1892a)—criteria that women would be more likely to adopt than men, and be more likely to seek in a candidate for office. Just the presence of females at polling places would inspire men to behave in a more serious and ethical manner, and even encourage them to moderate their speech; the experience of both Wyoming and the Isle of Man, where women have the right to vote, she argued, has demonstrated that this simple change produces a civilizing effect on men (Scott 1892a; "Womanhood Suffrage" 1892). Much as Rose Scott wished all women to have the ability to vote, she also expressed some skepticism about the significance of each woman personally casting a ballot, being very much aware that political decision-making owes a lot to lobbying; thus she was convinced that it was enfranchising women collectively that would allow them to have much more influence over the policies chosen (Scott 1892b). One concern expressed by Scott was what she felt was unfairness that "a boy of 21 years" was able to vote, while his mother could as yet not (Scott 1892d; "Womanhood Suffrage" 1892). Although Scott was understandably dismayed by the fact that women's lives were legally constricted beyond the ability to influence government, the apparent ageist refusal to concede adulthood to younger men, claiming dignity and humanity while denying it to others, seems a poor argument.

When Scott spoke about other matters—for example, in a lecture she gave on Sunday, April 24, 1892, at the Leichhardt Town Hall on "Marriage and Social Life," she pointed out that she was not speaking there in her role as a representative of the WSL. What she had to say about relationships, as recounted by the press, suggests a somewhat less radical understanding of the institution of marriage than that expressed by Rose Summerfield. Scott is reported as having said:

> The progress of humanity must begin with the individual, and men and women by discovering how they could live together in happiness and peace—in spite of their lower nature—discovered a principle which affected ages to come and the one which will gradually leaven the communities and nations on the earth and out of discord evoke harmony. . . . Fly not to remedies for social evils which were worse than the disease. ("'Marriage and Social Life': Lecture by Miss Rose Scott" 1892)

Elsewhere, Rose Summerfield (1895c), who advocated fixing the "social evils" that arose from marriage, presents more about this contemporary disjunction between Australian feminists through the medium of an imaginary debate between two women, Mrs. Welloff and Mrs. Workhard. Mrs. Welloff, who understands the cause as mainly being about obtaining the vote for women, is offended by the much wider agenda of Mrs. Workhard, who attaches the franchise issue to matters of poverty and property. It is not hard to see that Mrs. Workhard's arguments reveal the position of Summerfield, and it is quite possible that Mrs. Welloff is a caricature of Scott, who was wealthy enough never to have to take paid employment. A flattering portrait of Rose Scott in the Sydney area *Worker* described her as being "of a family, many members of which have held high and responsible positions in the colony" ("Miss Rose Scott: Hon. Secretary of the Womanhood Suffrage League of New South Wales" 1894). Whether or not Mrs. Welloff is intended to denote Rose Scott, it is clear that the women's movement in Australia is at an important crossroads here. In the United States, after the 19th Amendment to the US Constitution was passed in 1920, saying: "The right of citizens of the United States to vote shall not be denied or abridged by the United States or by any State on account of sex," most women's groups disbanded because they had achieved their goal, which was the franchise; much other progress on women's rights was thus delayed. Summerfield, via the character of Mrs. Workhard, is already in 1895 well apprized of the limitations that such a vote-focus will inflict and, the previous year, a column in the Brisbane *Worker* had observed:

> Mrs. Rose Summerfield is forcing the womanhood suffrage movement to the front in Sydney by Socialist arguments. Equal pay with men for equal work is her motto. ("Political" 1894)

She is also aware which groups she believes will be satisfied with achievement of the franchise, and which will most continue to suffer and therefore demur. "That magical bit of paper—the elector's right—will perhaps meet the requirements of a section of the suffragists, but what will it do for the majority of women workers?" (Summerfield 1895c). Moreover, Mrs. Workhard expresses dissatisfaction with its significance, lamenting the fact that, although most men can vote, this does not give them much say about how society is organized; thus Mrs. Welloff's argument that having a vote erects a balance in citizenship between the position of the "gentleman" and that of a unionized worker seems unlikely. While the Mrs. Workhard character concedes the necessity of focusing on the franchise issue to make progress, not scare some of its supporters away, and not be labeled a dangerous agitator, she points out that due to the ownership and control of land by capitalists, which prevents the majority of Australians from living on and working it, the issue of who votes will never fully address the question of who has rights (Summerfield 1895c).

Another instance of the way that the two Roses disagreed was that, while Rose Summerfield thought it was wrong for anyone under the age of 17 to be employed, and lamented the fact that girls were laboring in tough factory positions while some of their fathers were unable to find employment, she did not believe that raising the sexual age of consent, which at the time was 14 in New South Wales, would be effective as a means of preserving family life (Summerfield 1893a). Rose Scott, however, was successful at achieving this, in 1910, raising the legal age to 16.

At the root of Summerfield's position was skepticism about what often passed for democracy, the showy embrace of practices like voting on the part of cynical politicians whose real goal was to limit any significant participation in decision-making by the majority:

> [T]heir democracy is too often a figurehead that charlatans have gilded and dressed in spangled robes in order to mislead the unwary seeker after a higher order. The gilding and spangles deceive him, and he unfortunately becomes a puppet in the show, and progress stands a little longer still. (Summerfield 1898m)

This illusory democracy is wrapped up in legal principles and paperwork that constrict the ability of citizens not only to act as they wish, leaving many of them struggling to survive, but it also through its manipulations renders them unthinking, perplexingly satisfied dupes, who have no awareness of the true nature of their predicament (1898m).

> The goodness that is wanted to make Australia a land of plenty is not hall-marked by hungry politicians, amongst whom are included dividend drawers, usury bolsterers, calico Jimmies, bibulous dotards, "pretty Joey" members, each and all of whom profess to be ready to immolate themselves for their suffering country. No! a thousand times no. The Democracy of this scheming crew is the offspring of a vile corruption. (Summerfield 1898m)

The nature of politics is that those running for office make promises that appeal to ordinary people and thus they secure many of their votes but, Summerfield notes, their pledges are seldom fulfilled. Workers who are deceived in this way are often accepting of that failure because of the higher social position of those who are elected, an attraction which the politicians also take care to cultivate. Moreover, the ideology of voting seduces the poorest members of society, those only a paycheck away from starvation, into believing they are protected by the existence of an elected legislature, not realizing that "Parliament is a tool designed and carried out solely in the interests of the propertied classes" (Summerfield 1898s):

> You, Workman, with a vote in your possession, have imagined yourself sovereign; have fancied you had a say in ruling your country, in making its laws. You think now that you can redeem yourself from the position of wage slave or outcast, and your vote is recorded for the man you deem worthy to represent you. Your part of a public duty is carried out to the best of your ability, and, lo! instead of good and wise laws being the outcome, what have we but the steady increase of poverty amongst your class? (Summerfield 1898s)

But, she warns, eventually the repeated manipulation of voters by the political class will have to come to an end as more and more of those who have been bamboozled start to realize how the system really works (Summerfield 1898n).

Nevertheless, despite her lukewarm commitment to voting and awareness of its deceptive function, Rose Summerfield worked tirelessly on behalf of the women's suffrage campaign, demonstrating her oratorial excellence. When a public meeting of the WSL was held at the YMCA Hall in Sydney on November 8, 1893, completely filling the auditorium, and notwithstanding the disturbance caused by several hecklers, her speech in favor of allowing women to vote was praised by the chairperson of the meeting, former NSW premier Sir Henry Parkes, as being a performance that "in cultured eloquence, in keenness of reason, and in power of thought it would adorn any parliament in the world" ("Personal" 1893; "Women's Suffrage Meeting" 1893). Many attendees signed a petition to the colony parliament that night, asking for the extension of voting rights to women ("Womanhood Suffrage: Addresses by Sir Henry Parkes and Mr. Bruce Smith" 1893; "Women's Suffrage League: Three Lady Orators" 1893; "Women's Suffrage Meeting" 1893). At this point, women in the colony of New Zealand had succeeded in winning the vote, and Rose proposed the resolution, which was passed unanimously, "That this meeting heartily congratulates the people of New Zealand on being the first among Australians to obtain the franchise for the women of the colony" ("Womanhood Suffrage: Addresses by Sir Henry Parkes and Mr. Bruce Smith" 1893; "Woman's Suffrage" 1893). Lady Mary Elizabeth Windeyer, the president, and cofounder with Rose Scott, of the WSL, was also the leader of the franchise department of the Woman's Christian Temperance Union (WCTU), and a few weeks later, that organization held a meeting at Sydney's Temperance Hall which unanimously approved a similar motion proposed by Lady Windeyer, "That this meeting send its heartfelt congratulations to the women of New Zealand upon obtaining the franchise, and also upon the successful manner in which they organised their forces in the late general election" (Radi 1990; "Womanhood Suffrage" 1893). In April 1895, when Sir Henry Parkes chaired another meeting at Temperance Hall, he conceded that "I am not here as a total abstainer" (The Flaneur 1895), an occurrence that prompted a *Freeman's Journal* columnist to satirize Sir Henry's possible tendency to drink to excess, suggesting that the politician might previously have been more sincerely promoting his own career than committing himself to Rose Summerfield's WSL rhetoric:

> I don't think Parkes has filled a public meeting chair . . . since the night that my gifted gritty friend Mrs. Summerfield significantly said to her Woman Suffrage sisters, "When we select a male leader to champion our cause let us choose a man of unimpeachable morals." "Meanin' Me, of course," said Sir 'Enry sweetly, as he winked with the other eye; but I notice that he hasn't been very enthusiastic over the baggy-breeched movement since. The stern array of sharp-pointed ginghams in the front seats probably prevented the slippery old knight from saying. "Hi 'ave great pleasure in taking the chair, though Hi ham not 'ere as a hadvocate of puttin' women into pantaloons and Parliament." (The Flaneur 1895)

MARRIAGE AND SOCIAL CHANGE

The November 8, 1893, meeting also attracted the attention of John Haynes, a backer of household suffrage: from his perspective, men had the vote, and in exercising it, they spoke for their whole family (Haynes 1893a). Therefore, he claimed, since public policy has no actual need of female suffrage, and "marriage is the goal, or main object of a woman's life" (Haynes 1893b; 1893a is similar), then, if instead women sought to participate in society or politics independently of their husbands, they should be willing to forgo, and lose the ability to sue to obtain, the financial and moral support that they were presently guaranteed from the man they had married, and even lose any physical protection that a husband might provide in the event of an attack (Haynes 1893a, 1893b).

Maybanke S. Wolstenholme, who had become the new president of the WSL, responded to Haynes's argument saying that few people accepted his claim that "marriage is the goal of woman's existence" (Wolstenholme 1893). Not all women were confined to the home, and those who worked outside it or were involved in charitable pursuits needed to be educated in the ways of the outside world. Individuals often disagreed with each other, and many times that disagreement was appropriate, so it was unreasonable to allow men to make all the decisions when some of them may be wrong; moreover, placing power in the hands of men undermined the rights of single women, who lacked husbands (Wolstenholme 1893):

> Humanity is made up of men and women, separate entities, individuals, each with its own physical, mental, and spiritual peculiarities and no one person can represent or take the responsibility of another; especially a man cannot represent a woman, because the sexes are naturally different in all that relates to external life. (Wolstenholme 1893)

Responding in a subsequent letter to the editor to Wolstenholme's arguments, Haynes argued "that the lady president and her friends know little of the terrible struggle for existence among even the strongest men in that outside world, into whose turmoil they seek to push weak woman" (Haynes 1893b). Haynes argued that if the desires of the WSL were to be implemented, "if she is to meet man on all equality, she will find the world too cold and cruel to allow her to define her own avocations or her own remuneration. Woman has no robustness of nature, and surely, Mrs Wolstenholme knows the physical distracting infirmities of her own sex" (Haynes 1893b).

Also contributing to the discussion, though less politely, a woman who signed herself "M." asked Haynes whether he was seeking to advance Mormonism by having men marry the million "extra" women who presently had no one upon whom to rely; surely, M. responded, human civilization can rise above the level of "a rabbit-warren" (M. 1893):

> If marriage—i.e., reproduction—were the goal of civilised men and women, we should be nothing higher than ephemera. (M. 1893)

At this point, Rose Summerfield entered the fray with another piece in the *Sydney Morning Herald*, in which she questioned the existence of the ignorance that Haynes had attributed to women about aspects of life in the real world, and which therefore apparently ruled them ineligible to participate in political decision-making, even though, she was sure, most people in the world were unhappy with the way that their lives were governed, and they had been governed for the past century by men (Summerfield 1893d). Rather than women being ignorant, she argued:

> [K]nowing the dreadful conditions that exist in the industrial world, making the struggle for a livelihood severer every year, we have the sense to see and know that the same cruel conditions weigh heavily upon both sexes alike and that therefore there exists an urgent necessity for women to step out of their retirement and take up the cudgels on behalf of not women alone, but suffering humanity, thus giving prominence to the recognition of the indissoluble tie that binds the sexes. (Summerfield 1893d)

In fact, Rose's awareness of life in the city and its profound failure to offer a decent life to most residents suggests that she had a more accurate understanding of social problems than many of the male politicians who had so far held on to power. She points out that, despite their physical disadvantages, women often work in the outside world just as hard as men do, but employers, including the state, are allowed to pay them less, simply because of their gender (Summerfield 1893d). Notably, many of the constraints she identifies that limit the improvement of human civilization remain, more than a hundred years later, in the present world, where the majority suffers unnecessarily.

> [W]e see the children of the poor being forced into idleness, and watch them growing into larrikins and loafers, denied a place in society except as denizens of the vile slums, congregated with criminals; because the avenues of honest employment are closed through the reign of monopoly and the fierce competition of hand and brain workers, who are not allowed to earn a decent living. (Summerfield 1893d)

On the other hand, returning to her older position, Rose points out that, like Haynes, she does not believe that women ought to work in every kind of employment, and that this remains a matter of divergence between herself and some of her WSL colleagues:

> I am sorry, indeed, to have to admit that some women who like to pose as advance guards in the reform movement advocate that women workers should follow the plough, clear land, become bootmakers, carpenters, &c. With these I have no sympathy whatever, and will gladly leave them to Mr. Haynes's strongest criticism. (Summerfield 1893d)

In fact, Wolstenholme's argument that not many people regarded the statement that "marriage is the goal of woman's existence" as being true might at times have encountered some skepticism on the part of her ally, Rose Summerfield. In an article titled "Present Day Problems" (Summerfield 1898j), Rose writes:

> How strong is the desire for motherhood in many women; the intense yearning for the touch of baby fingers, the longings to fold a tiny bud of Godhead to their breast. It is apart, altogether apart, from sensuality. It in reality is the woman's "will to live," and is at once the crown and glory of her being. (Summerfield 1898j)

Rose refers to the will to survive and perpetuate the species that exists in all natural forms, but which, she argues, has not been adequately studied in women, some of whom are presently even medicated to repress desires and feelings of unhappiness that do not fit well with the contradictory needs of a capitalistic society. Denied many of the rights enjoyed by men, women who want to openly reveal their natural desires are silenced by society, while their bodies may be physically or mentally damaged by working hard in oppressive, crowded factories and other forms of "artificial living" (1898j). Throughout their childhoods, they are educated for subservience, and taught to behave in an unnatural, cloistered manner in a way that serves the interests of others, rather than being allowed to operate in a style that conforms to their natural heritage:

> These are the fundamental teachings of the social and religious laws—repression and obedience—and one can assert without fear of contradiction that this teaching is justly responsible for the artificiality and dissimulation with which the sex are so often charged. (Summerfield 1898j)

To overcome this predicament, Rose continues, there must be societal change, movement away from the dogmas of economics in favor of a new sort of enlightenment to which "Churchianity cannot in any way contribute" (1898j), in order to better incorporate people's natural needs and goals and each person's right to share fairly the fruits of their labor. Perhaps revealing her hopes for such a new, idealistic type of existence in one of the "New Australia" settlements in Paraguay to which she will, the following year, relocate, and where she will have four more children, she writes:

> [T]here is a great hope ahead for a re-adjustment of society, in which "the will to live," that so strongly animates human beings, will receive no brutal checks sanctioned by law and religion. (Summerfield 1898j)

If the basic conditions under which people conduct their lives are improved, with the poor finally having enough to eat, then the relative comfort will cause them to reflect more on the conditions they presently take for granted, making them more likely to want to behave in an ethical manner and to be better informed, which in turn will hopefully make them more knowledgeable about the economic power they in reality possess as consumers who are also workers (Summerfield 1898q). Sounding like Kropotkin (1924, 28), she continued:

> We all know that a sculler or wrestler has better chest development, consequently stronger muscles in his arms, back, etc., than the clerk who stoops over a desk eight or nine hours a day wielding a pen; so also is it quite easy to understand that people who have leisure to study reach a higher intellectual stage than the toil-worn, uncultured wage-earner. (Summerfield 1898q)

Thinking about a more logical and fair way of organizing the workplace would be sure to bring about improvement, and unionized women being paid a more reasonable wage could participate in this process; since Rose had already set up a cooperative laundry, it is not surprising that she suggests this as an example where enhancements could be achieved:

> If a few earnest women, sincere in their endeavor to ease the burdens laid upon their weaker sisters, would take up this idea of co-operation it could very soon be carried into effect without a very great outlay. A co-operative laundry run on principles, well directed, judiciously advertised and canvassed for amongst sympathisers would very soon gain favor and patronage. (Summerfield 1898q)

Indeed, Summerfield was in general quite successful at linking her concern for ordinary workers with her feminist goals. In a piece in the Sydney area *Worker* on November 26, 1892, she reported on events at a meeting of the AWU at Sydney's Protestant Hall that she had chaired. She emphasized the message of another of the participants, AWU leader W. G. Spence, that women in particular could derive significant benefit from joining the union, given that women were often employed in home-based piece-rate types of employment. At the same meeting, a woman called Mrs. Jenkins, who had seven children, described her difficulty attempting to find work in the current circumstances. The union gathering then proceeded to discuss the potential benefits of setting up a residential facility for female workers, where daycare could be provided, lessening the disadvantage affecting persons such as Mrs. Jenkins (Summerfield 1892h). Of course, the need to access daycare facilities remains a largely unsolved problem today that continues to undermine women's quest for equal rights.

In 1894, notwithstanding all her various other activities, Rose found time to speak at public meetings on street corners in favor of candidates she liked, such as the GLU/AWU vice president, Thomas J. Tytherleigh ("General Laborers' Union of Australasia" 1893; "Mr. Tytherleigh's Candidature" 1894a, 1894b; "The Shearing Difficulty: Work Proceeding Quietly" 1894). By 1898, Rose Summerfield was continuing to advocate female suffrage while also emphasizing the need for unions, as well as the limited latitude to be expected from voting due to the actual nature of Parliament, which in practice made the exaggerated claims of democratic theory open to doubt:

> The legislative machinery is cumbersome and difficult to set in motion, especially when one considers the remarkable power of veto possessed by the aptly-termed fossilized Upper House. (Summerfield 1898q)

Stressing the reason why she continued to campaign for the vote for women even though her commitment did not arise from confidence that its achievement would prove to be the magic key that opened the door to social change, she wrote:

> I demand the vote for women—not because I think society will be regenerated by its use, but as a right which should not be denied them. Parliament is really a mighty palavering shop, and does not in any way institute reform; it merely sanctions and passes into law what the people make the strongest demand for: Not the most humane or intelligent, but things advocated by those who are temporarily the strongest. (Summerfield 1898a)

Nonetheless, although successful true reform awaited the exercise of education and ingenuity, the political apparatus might be used to bring about some changes desired by women, because the increased attention of politicians around election time to those wishes, a modification which would follow the extension of the franchise, could make some limited victories more likely to happen. Ironically, she continues, hunger not only inflicts unhappiness and social instability onto human beings, but it also gives birth to political extremism. Rose was ever concerned about the negative effects of having to toil long and hard as a part of an unnatural existence, most people having little time to sit and contemplate, to rest awhile, and so they become unhappy and fail to appreciate the value of beauty, health, and freedom, as the profit made from ordinary workers' industry goes mostly to the wealthy (Summerfield 1896c). In her poem, "Be True to Self," she refers to the damage, mental and physical, that afflicted many of the workers around her in Sydney and beyond:

> Maimed in the struggle and strain,
> Slaving for others to reap;
> Building for idlers who gain
> The riches yourself should keep. (Summerfield 1898b)

If, on the other hand, the working classes enjoyed more comforts, they would have greater opportunity to consider in a reasoning way how labor was organized, and start to recognize the desire of politicians to maintain the dominance of "capitalism against the working classes, the pitting of money against the brains and sinews of an already oppressed people" (Summerfield 1898a). Within that existing framework, the main role of Parliament was actually to appear to be a democratic instrument of representation when, in reality, it was "a big, unwieldly fetish before which men prostrate themselves, a mere abstraction hemmed in with a lot of lawyer's phrases" (1898a). Instead, the exercise of pressure for more widespread reform than simply the right to vote, spread through the medium of an organized labor movement, would be much more likely to succeed (1898a):

> Know, this, workers of N.S.W.—whether you are in the desk or the counting-house, the factory or the back-block station, or you women behind counters, at noisy machines in factories, or typewriting in offices—that a fair share of this leisure, this pleasure and treasure, is yours as soon as ever you are intellectually strong enough to demand them; as soon as ever you form a combination against commercial despotism. (Summerfield 1898a)

Thus, as in her poem, "Here and Now" (Summerfield 1898f), she encouraged others to press for social change rather than waiting for some later, more auspicious moment that may never arrive:

> Not the future—sister, brother,
> Do not to that mirage bow;
> This our moment—there's none other
> Wants our help so much as Now. (Summerfield 1898f)

Seeking to combine two of her interests, Summerfield gave a lecture on January 26, 1896, called "Women's Place in the Temperance Movement" at the Protestant Hall in Sydney before members of the Good Templars

Mission, a single-issue organization that promoted abstinence from alcohol. Explaining why she had only recently become a supporter of the group, she said that, although she had always shared their concerns regarding the use of alcohol, in the past she had felt some of their activism to be overzealous, but she was now of the opinion that because of the social problems caused by the presence of alcohol in the community, it was time for various organizations to try and work together cooperatively. Within a few weeks, as reported at the Templary's subsequent annual meeting, Rose had been installed as an officer of the metropolitan district lodge ("Good Templar Mission" 1896; "Good Templary" 1896; Hearn 2004, 77; "I.O.G.T." 1896).

Chapter 3

Freethinker and Political Theorist

SECULARISM

In 1885, Rose attended the Australasian Secularist Association's (ASA) meetings at the Hall of Science in the Fitzroy area of Melbourne that were held with some sense of irony on Sundays, and this is where she encountered Joseph Symes. She soon became one of the association's teachers. Prior to her arrival in Melbourne, she was involved with the ASA branch in Ballarat, Vic., and she seems to have encountered some prejudice there due to her freethinking opinions, losing friends and being called names by persons she encountered in the street. Rose's connection to Symes continued after she moved to Sydney. An advertisement in the *Liberator* indicated that additional copies of Symes's periodical could be obtained for 3s. 6d per quarter prepaid from its "Sydney Agents; New South Wales Branch Australasian Secular Association, over Summerfield's Tailoring Establishment, Pitt-street," which appears to be the residence of Rose and tailor husband Henry Summerfield ("Death of Rose Summerfield" 1922; Hearn 2003, 257, 2004, 68; James 1986; "The Pamphlet Collection of Sir Robert Stout: Volume 82" N.d.; Smith 1963, 37).

Symes had arrived in Melbourne from England in 1884 to serve as the ASA's organizer and, in addition to his meeting and educational activities, he purchased a printing press and started to produce the *Liberator*, a weekly publication to promote secular views that encountered much opposition, and was prosecuted by the colony government as well as sued by the Lord's Day Observance Society. In addition to mocking Christianity and the bible, Symes referred to capital punishment as "judicial murder" (Smith 1963, 32). The ASA had been founded in 1882 and opponents started immediately to try to close down its activities (Smith 1963, 26, 32, 34–35, 1976).

As a secularist, Rose Summerfield took the view that the influence of religious teachings and of religious persons was in decline and appropriately so. Insofar as people such as herself were involved with organizing workers or women, she wanted pious talk to be completely excised from the coordinating process. While she accepted that everyone should have liberty to believe whatever they wished, using traditional Christian arguments to make the case for improving working conditions might ultimately undermine the development of their cause. Rather, she said, "I firmly believe that when girls and women are once got together the religion of humanity will awaken in their breasts and quite supersede the old superstition" (Summerfield 1892e).

In "Christmas, 1896" (Summerfield 1896b), Summerfield contrasts the poverty experienced and addressed by Jesus and the simplicity and goodness of the words attributed to him with the contemporary wealth of churches in Australia and around the world that today profess allegiance to the same teachings, but do so in front of affluent congregations as though the promise and pious goals of Christianity have already been achieved. Meanwhile:

> Within a stones [*sic*] throw of these stately edifices, aye in their very shadow, the sun rays glinted through smeared windowpanes on beings that never know peace; the face of God and the hand of man is ever against them. They toiled, but the earth-lords had the fullness of their industry, They were weak, and the strong most cruelly oppressed them. They erred, but none were merciful to them. They pleaded for God's law, but man's law mocked and reviled them. (Summerfield 1896b)

As long as many remain landless, exposed to the extortion of landlords who profit from property they have no right to own, and as long as there are orphans, and women must sacrifice their virtue to survive, with deprivation being widespread, then Christianity, Rose argues, will have failed to achieved the successes it claims.

> "And God so loved the world that he gave his only begotten son to die for it." Oh! what a lie, a vile monstrous lie the many are living! What hypocrisy they practise? Their god is the demon of cant and his son is usury; he is living and thriving, and his victims are perishing by thousands. The God of love is dethroned and a golden image raised in his stead. (Summerfield 1896b)

In another piece, "The Earth is the Lord's and the Fullness Thereof" (Summerfield 1896d), Rose explores the same idea, taking a sentence from the bible (it occurs at 1 Corinthians 10:26 and in Psalm 24:1), contrasting the beauty of Nature and life in the countryside:

> He thought of the city he had left, where houses were huddled together—so close that the sun's rays rarely lit the cheerless rooms; the inmates [*sic*] lives were dull, and cold, and comfortless; the little children had the stunted, hard look that these wretched houses, narrow streets, dirty lanes, and coarse fare imparts to our unfortunate species. (Summerfield 1896d)

Similarly, in her poem, "Dreams and Seems" (Summerfield 1898e), Rose emphasizes the shallowness of Christian ambitions and achievements:

> I ain't got much religion, perhaps;
> You see it never come my way—
> The gaitered, well-paid, swellish chaps,
> Don't work like Christ did in his day—
> P'raps *Christ* was dreamin' too.
> If God made heav'n, an' earth, an' man,
> Some orful rich, some beastly poor;
> I hope he'll alter that bad plan,
> Such work as that it can't endure,
> Unless in *seemin'* too.
> So if things are not what they seem,
> I wish our eyes 'ud see the right;
> 'Taint good to live in one long dream
> With hunger pangs from morn till night—
> Such *dreams* make men feel blue. (Summerfield 1898e)

In her poem, "My Baptism," Summerfield (1898h) challenges the common belief among Christians that without faith, human beings will be unable to behave morally. In contradistinction, she points out that, unlike some believers, she has personally helped out victims of poverty, rather than denigrating or ignoring them; she has not stolen other people's money, or sexually assaulted anyone, or pressed people to return money they owed. Elsewhere, she questions the motives of the Salvation Army for operating a public baths and flophouse in Sydney where they "are running it on purely commercial lines, but, of course, parade it under the guise of charity" (1899b). She, on the other hand, despite the alleged ethical incapability imposed by being a freethinker, has never taken advantage of others in an exploitative way:

> I was never known in the best of days
> To sweat my "hands" till I earned their curse;
> To give them bibles and tell them to praise
> God, while I further emptied their purse. (Summerfield 1898h)

Anyway, it may turn out, she continues, that if the claims of an afterlife are correct, doing right according to one's own values and experience, notwithstanding the fact that this is a haphazard process constituting a baptism of "water unblessed," it is possible that, "If Christ is there he my ticket will fix" (1898h). Here, Rose has implicitly rejected Blaise Pascal's ([1670] 1849) assumption of a need to make a wager on the existence of God; for her, the element of choice lies instead with the individual, who decides how she will live her own life, and she may not lose ultimately by doing so:

> Contented am I to toss for a chance!
> And if I cut trumps there's part of my life
> That's led the devil full many a dance,
> That'll help me over the gulf of strife. (Summerfield 1898h)

ANARCHIST INFLUENCES

The fate of the Chicago anarchists of the Haymarket Tragedy quickly came to prominence among the concerns of many radicals around the world and was clearly dear to the heart of Rose Summerfield. On May 4, 1886, there was an attempt to close a large public meeting, the day after several strikers from the McCormick Reaper Works in Chicago had been shot by police, and more than 2,000 people now gathered to protest. Someone threw a bomb, killing an officer, Mathias J. Degan, and eight local anarchists were arrested and charged with murder. Following an unfair and much-flawed trial, all eight were found guilty, and four of them were hanged, an event now and then much criticized as an instance of judicial murder (Avrich 1980, i-ii, 1984; DeLamotte 2004, 4–5; Shone 2013, ch. 5). On November 13, 1898, Rose gave a lecture at Mayfield Hall, home of the Australian Socialist League, called "Who, Being Dead, Yet Speaketh." She began by reciting "To the Reformers of England," a poem by John Greenleaf Whittier, which one of the Haymarket anarchists, Albert Parsons, had delivered shortly before he was executed ("Notes and Comments" 1898; "The Chicago Anarchists" 1898.) The poem contains the lines:

> The good which bloodshed could not gain
> Your peaceful zeal shall find.
> Press on! the triumph shall be won
> Of common rights and equal laws. (Whittier [1843] 1997)

As paraphrased by the *Worker* reporter, Summerfield told the meeting:

> Truly, we are a policemanized community, and as long as this overweening respect or rather abject fear of a policeman or jack-in-office exists we have small chance of getting any beneficial change in our social system. Anarchy literally means 'without rulership'; its disciples desire to agitate for liberty and freedom. And if the numerous outrages attributed to them were traced to their proper source, it would be found that in most cases the police had more to do with them than the Anarchists." ("The Chicago Anarchists" 1898)

Interestingly, in the light of Rose's prior involvement with Joseph Symes and the Australasian Secularist Association (ASA), it was David A. Andrade of the Melbourne Anarchist Club (MAC), which had split from Symes and the ASA, who consistently wrote in favor of the Chicago martyrs. As Smith notes, some MAC members, "[Frederic] Upham, [J. A.] Andrews and [Larry] Petrie strongly supported the Chicago anarchists and their policy of violence" (Smith 1963, 43). Amid the strikes of the early 1890s, Petrie, full name Laurence de Petrie and also known as George Frederick Howard, who had been born in Scotland and who briefly worked with Rose Summerfield at the GLU/AWU, and eventually, like her, emigrated to the Cosme settlement in Paraguay, was accused of attempting in July 1893 to blow up a non-union steamship, the *Aramac*. Petrie credited his acquittal to the assistance that Rose now provided on his case (Burgmann 1985a, 32; James 1999; Lane [1939] 1993, 67–68; "Outrage on the Aramac" 1893; Souter [1968] 2012, 156; "The Aramac Explosion" 1893; "The Explosion on the Aramac" 1893; Whitehead [1997] 2018, 814).

Symes, on the other hand, appeared to change his mind, at first showing support for the Chicago anarchists in the *Liberator* of May 16, 1888, but later spreading misinformation about the accused, and expressing his approval of their hangings, which was also an about-turn in his position on capital punishment (Vandelaar 1985). In the MAC's journal, *Honesty*, Andrade (1888) pointed out the reality of the situation, which is now generally accepted by scholars:

> The trial, from beginning to end, was a mockery of justice. The perjured evidence of paid liars was received for the prosecution, and witnesses for the defence were refused a hearing. (Andrade 1888, 74)

Andrade's comments were confirmed in 1893 by Illinois Governor John P. "Pete" Altgeld when he pardoned the three accused who had not been executed or committed suicide:

> [M]uch of the evidence given at the trial was a pure fabrication. . . . [S]ome of the prominent police officials, in their zeal, not only terrorized ignorant men by throwing them into prison and threatening them with torture if they refused to swear to anything desired, . . . they offered money and employment to those who would consent to do this. (Altgeld [1893] 1915, 304–305)

Some years earlier, on Thursday, August 4, 1892, Summerfield had participated in an event at Sydney's School of Arts to celebrate the centenary of the death of the atheist and philosophical anarchist poet, Percy Bysshe Shelley, in which she recited his poem, "Address to the Lord Chancellor," no doubt identifying strongly with the poet's damning of the hypocrisy of political leaders and judges; among those present was the gathering's chairperson and opening speaker, Edmund "Toby" Barton, the current acting premier of NSW and future High Court of Australia justice and initial prime minister of Australia. In her "Master and Man" speech, Rose had quoted from Shelley's "Masque of Anarchy" ("Shelley's Centenary: Celebration at the School of Arts" 1892; Summerfield 1892b, 3). However, while Shelley in his poem about the Peterloo massacre advocated a response of nonviolent resistance which has influenced many, including Mahatma Gandhi, Rose also in that same "Master and Man" performance turned his message around, quoting some of Shelley's "Lines Written During the Castlereagh Administration" (Shelley 1819–1820), instead characterizing passive resistance as quiet surrender:

> So, you see, most of the work is waiting to be done. Who is going to do it? Who will take it in hand? Must it be left to one or two, or will you still say in Shelley's words:
>
> Then trample and dance thou oppressor [in the original, Oppressor],
> For thy victim is no redressor [redresser];
> Thou art sole lord and possessor
> Of her corpses, her clods, and abortions—they pave
> Thy path to the grave. (Summerfield 1892b, 8)

Shelley has inspired many admirers, including William Lane's brother, Ernie, who wrote in his autobiography:

> Of all these seers and prophets of the Future's Day, when "All will be better than well"—Shelley was the greatest—and the best beloved. (Lane [1939] 1993, 29)

Barton, as acting premier and attorney general, had been involved in undermining the Broken Hill strike and in arresting some of the miners, and the fact that he was participating in the celebration of Shelley struck Ernie and his brothers as being particularly galling, although Ernie recalls that a letter he sent to Sydney's *Daily Telegraph* to complain about it was not printed (Lane [1939] 1993, 55–57). Summerfield, on the other hand, was ever a practitioner of speaking truth to power, and she may have felt more could be achieved by attending and confronting those with whom she strongly disagreed, rather than by attempting to silence them.

Bob James, the chronicler of anarchism in Australia, considers Rose to be an anarchist, noting, for instance that "[o]ther secularists who went from the ASA to play prominent parts in anarchist history included John William

"Chummy" Fleming, Rose Stone, William McNamara and John Andrews" (James 1986). In fact, other aspects of her thought are quite consonant with anarchist perspectives: for instance, her desire to create a workforce that operated without bosses; her interest and that of her second husband in the ideas of Henry George and the single tax movement; her related desire for land reform so that ordinary people could possess their own land and use it to farm; her skepticism about the value of voting and its allegedly "democratic" credentials; and her eventual relocation to a communitarian settlement in Paraguay could all be considered expressions of an anarchist viewpoint. Moreover, her Alexander Berkman-like concern to awaken ordinary people from their passive acceptance of the way society and its "democracy" are organized, inciting them, as she did in her "Master and Man" speech, to insist upon better treatment, fits well with the characterization of her at least to some extent as an anarchist thinker. She wanted liberty for herself and for each family, and in her "The Gospel of Discontent" performance, she discusses the lack of free time which afflicts most workers to the extent that they have little opportunity to appraise the reality of their situation or develop their own talents and interests, a perspective that brings to mind that of Peter Kropotkin. Like Kropotkin, she wished to reorganize the way that land was used to benefit ordinary people who lived in cities. The alternative of the workhouse, on the other hand, she deems a repressive institution of the state. Her idea that idlers and bosses should be helping the community with the work is compatible with Kropotkin and Lucy Parsons and other anarchists who have pointed out that the number of hours each person needs to work would be much less if society were organized more appropriately: for example, maybe work would be necessary only for persons aged 25–45, and for just twenty hours a week (Kropotkin ([1906] 1990, 192; Parsons 2004, 35).

SOCIALISM

Despite the affinity of some of Summerfield's views with anarchism, she advocated socialist ideas and she was an active member of the Australian Socialist League (ASL). She was not a communist, although, as indicated above, Rose demonstrated in some of her speeches an informal familiarity with the ideas of false consciousness, alienated labor, and creation of surplus value; often, her ideas resemble those of John Stuart Mill, with whom she was familiar, and of Labor/Social Democrat parties in general (Bowden 2011, 57). The exception is the idea of the state owning all or all large businesses, controlling the means of production, an idea which occurs in her writings and speeches, and here she perhaps most resembles the utopian vision of Edward Bellamy. In his once more influential science fiction bestseller, *Looking Backward: 2000–1887* (Bellamy 1887), copies of which his one-time admirer, William Lane, had as part of his ALF duties circulated in Queensland, where there was a "Bellamy Club," Bellamy presented a view of a perfect socialistic society, avoiding the word socialism, which, like Rose, he saw as having negative connotations, and instead referring to what he advocated as nationalism. Many of the problems faced by those at the end of the nineteenth century no longer exist in Bellamy's ideal imagined world of 2000 in its well-planned cities: private property, poverty and classes, crime, and war no longer limit people's opportunities to live their lives as they wish (Beaumont 2007; Ross 1947, 112; Stewart 1972, xi). Recreation is much more available, while paid work is limited, as Kropotkin, Lucy Parsons, and other anarchists had envisaged, to a specific section of people's lives, with the workers themselves selecting their professions; in the state portrayed in *Looking Backward*, work is necessary only between the ages of 21 and 45 (Bellamy 1887, ch. VI) . . . but it cannot be evaded.

However, while Bellamy's criticism of the way the world is organized in the late nineteenth century is, with the advantage of hindsight, easily justifiable, the solution he proffers is much less easy to evaluate or support. Tarnoff, for example, writes:

> The future produced nearly the opposite of what Bellamy had hoped. Large-scale social engineering led not only to utopian dreams but to genocides. (Tarnoff 2011)

Though Bellamy presents women in 2000 as possessing equal rights and opportunities, in his portrayal they retain their rather distinctive social roles compared with those of men; as Nelson (2019) points out, not every aspect of *Looking Backward* could accurately anticipate societal change, so in terms of women's rights, its ideal world of the future seems to actually be stuck in the past. Moreover, Bellamy's desire for a highly stratified social system in which labor is organized with a militaristic efficiency, where "A man able to do duty, and persistently refusing, is sentenced to solitary imprisonment on bread and water till he consents" (Bellamy 1887, ch. XII) and citizens are constantly watched and evaluated by their leaders, being promoted or demoted frequently on the basis of their commitment to society's goals, suggests the kind of future experienced once in East Germany from which many risked or gave their lives to escape, and nothing like the prosperity of the West was ever achieved despite the widespread predominance of government control and citizen surveillance. Part of the problem here, for Bellamy, and also for Summerfield and Lane, is that, the more the state controls the economy, ordinary people seem to lose their ability to complain or to suggest enhancements or to be left alone. Would efficiency really be improved by Bellamy's apparent solution, or would the economy just slow down, no longer able to respond to market pressures as bureaucracy ballooned outward, affecting every aspect of human existence? Would innovation disappear? Bellamy glibly assumes that the size of the resulting organism will mandate its greater success, criticizing the way that the economy is organized in his own time:

> People would be prompt enough to ridicule an army in which there were neither companies, battalions, regiments, brigades, divisions, or army corps,—no unit of organization, in fact, larger than the corporal's squad, with no officer higher than a corporal, and all the corporals equal in authority. And yet just such an army were the manufacturing industries of nineteenth century Boston, an army of four thousand independent squads led by four thousand independent corporals, each with a separate plan of campaign. (Bellamy 1887, ch. XXVII)

Instead, he presents a superior world where a "Great Trust" has swallowed up the product of all the previous mergers, ending capitalism and facilitating the "nationalist" state. Summerfield's goal in also desiring such a "Great Trust," though she did not use that nomenclature, in seeking substantial control of the economy by the state, is to improve the quality of life for everybody. Bellamy wrote:

> The industry and commerce of the country, ceasing to be conducted by a set of irresponsible corporations and syndicates of private persons at their caprice and for their profit, were intrusted to a single syndicate representing the people, to be conducted in the common interest for the common profit. The nation, that is to say, organized as the one great business corporation in which all other corporations were absorbed; it became the one capitalist in the place of all other capitalists, the sole employer, the final monopoly in which all previous and lesser monopolies were swallowed up, a monopoly in the profits and economies of which all citizens shared. The epoch of trusts had ended in The Great Trust. (Bellamy 1887, ch. V)

A report that appeared in a number of newspapers in the United States and elsewhere, itself based on a visit to Colonia Cosme by a German journalist, Wilhelm Lacmann, was quick to make a comparison with Bellamy's envisaged utopia:

> A community which closely approximates Bellamy's "Looking Backward" is Cosme, a little settlement near Asuncion, Paraguay. . . . Equality, democracy and community of wealth and work are the principles on which it was founded in 1894 by a split in a colony of Austrian [*sic*] immigrants to Paraguay. ("Odd Colony in Paraguay" 1905)

Some of the other newspapers that ran this report also printed it with the mistaken "Austrian" identity, while others corrected it to "Australian" (for example, "The Latest Utopia: A 'Looking Backward' Town" 1905). Harvey surely exaggerates the influence of Bellamy when, misspelling the title of Bellamy's book, he writes:

> Inspired by Edward Bellamy's utopian vision outlined in his popular novel of the time, *Looking Backwards*, Lane led an expedition of two hundred ambitious souls to the shores of Paraguay in the *Royal Tar* in 1893. (Harvey 2010, 299)

Instead, it is the example of Cosme, at the point at which that colony has survived for nine years, and not New Australia or its founders' creative imaginings, that leads Black (1903) to suggest it as a possible counterexample to the rule that "the various communal societies and experimental communities that grew out of 'Looking Backward'" generally lack "that persistence which would entitle them to be regarded as serious experiments on which a complete scheme could be built." Meanwhile, the initial Australian exodus from Paraguay was interpreted in a report in an Idaho newspaper as being a reflection on the appropriateness of Bellamy's views:

> Pilgrims are constantly returning from the new Australian colony in Paraguay. They say that an attempt was made to start a model settlement founded on the teachings of Bellamy, but that instead, the whole settlement was run by the devil. The sufferings of members of the Australian colony are terrible. ("Woe and Trouble in Australia" 1895)

From the perspective of those on the political left, the creation of a Labor Party in the Australian colonies, which would soon, in 1901, merge into a single entity, forced its leaders and supporters to decide whether it should serve the working people and their unions and their specific interests, or if it should be the agent of a wider mass of people. The Labor Party had grown out of the Great Strikes, although scholars continue to debate the causes of those disputes, the relative importance of different factors, and their significance for Antipodean history (Svensen 1995, xiv–xv). In Queensland, the party's foundation by the striking shearers who met under the "Tree of Knowledge" in Barcaldine in 1891 and 1892—at least, its symbolic foundation, considering that a decision to do the same thing had been made at an earlier meeting of the ALF (Bowden 2009, 3, 10)—cemented the association of the party with the union interest, but to many the new party in practice seemed to have left that activism behind; for example, W. G. Spence, previously a leader of the enlargement and consciousness-building of union membership, now a Labor member of parliament, no longer saw himself as an agent of the working class

(Conrick 1979; Lane [1939] 1993, 61–62). Verity Burgmann takes the view that it was due to these types of concern that Rose eventually moved away from endorsing socialism:

> Summerfield, a strong-minded and strong-featured woman, had been in this period a convinced state socialist, believing that state ownership and control of the means of production, distribution and exchange, brought about by the action of the Labor Party in parliament, would bring about freedom, equality, prosperity and happiness for working people. By 1897, she had become totally disillusioned, not just with the Labor MPs themselves, but with the entire state socialist strategy. She left the Socialist League. (Burgmann 1985a, 32)

When Hearn (2005) writes in similar fashion that "she resigned from the A.S.L. in 1897, and bitterly lamented workmen who were 'gulled' by the 'mighty bribe' of suffrage," any skepticism about voting would not appear to indicate a deviation in her core beliefs. As noted in chapter 2, as she came to accept and embrace the WSL campaign for the vote for women, Rose had continued to emphasize her doubts that voting could be anything like as important as the other types of social change that she advocated. Some of her 1898 columns shared the skepticism of other union leaders that the Labor Party they had created would be able to serve many of their interests. However, she had never embraced every aspect or form of socialism: perhaps, rather than being viewed as having turned away from the ideas of the ASL, she can be seen as having always been fully committed to labor unionism, but not necessarily to every policy pursued by everyone with whom she interacted. She wrote:

> There may be, nay: there is much that is objectionable about some brands of Socialism; but in that form of Socialism that has for its single object the raising of the wage-slaves from their false and brutalising position there can be no mistake whatever. You needn't call it Socialism. It really does not want a name to recommend it; but, Workman, when it comes before your notice in the guise of Trades Unionism do not, if you value your salvation from injustice, on any account flout it. (Summerfield 1898s)

While Rose can be seen as having refocused from one interest to another—socialism in the early 1890s, chairing ASL meetings and representing that organization when she delivered speeches, participating in the single-tax movement in 1895, developing more interest in temperance advocacy in 1896, and turning into a more fervent feminist as she became more involved with her leadership activities at the Womanhood Suffrage League and adapted to its overarching goal of obtaining the vote for females—she embraced a range of progressive causes and union perspectives, not necessarily abandoning those other interests as she picked up another pursuit. One of her goals at the ASL was to encourage debate with those of other views, seeking to hold public debates with advocates of more individualist philosophies, and those with different opinions about the economy. For example, a Professor Anderson from the University of Sydney gave a lecture at an ASA meeting at Leigh House on Sunday, October 2, 1892, titled "Why I am not a Socialist" ("Australian Socialist League" 1892a; "Socialist League" 1892). Clearly, this tolerant, open-minded approach did not resemble what Rose (1898s) noted as constituting "much that is objectionable about some brands of Socialism." The existence of Leigh House alone offered Sydney area residents plenty of opportunities to participate or simply become aware of a range of radical and progressive activities.

Rose's interest in land reform led to her interest in the short-lived Single-Tax League (STL), a movement with which some of the Australian Shearers' Union (ASU) leaders were involved, although its ideas were not necessarily embraced by other advocates of political reform such as those who sought protectionist trade policies (Scates 1986, 72, 75, 81). Thus Summerfield could be found presenting a lecture on "Woman's Position and Destiny in Reform" at an STL meeting in Sydney on the evening of March 12, 1895, in which she emphasized the need to enable everyone "to produce the necessaries of life" ("Single-Tax League" 1895), apparently a corollary of land reform. In *Progress and Poverty*, Henry George, who visited Australia in 1889, had pioneered the idea of imposing a tax on the value of unused land as a means of opening up its ownership to a greater percentage of people (Ross 1947, 112). This strategy, he argued, was likely to be effective because, unlike other taxes, which could be passed on to product consumers, thus avoiding payment of the taxes by the person or organization who was actually the target of the levy, a single tax would have to be paid by the landowner, which, George contended, would force the sale of some of the land, opening it up for use by others. Without such an approach, governments would continue to raise money using different taxes, which directly or indirectly impoverished ordinary wage-earners and benefited the wealthy, who were of course opposed to implementation of the single tax:

> The ingenuity of statesmen has been exercised in devising schemes of taxation which drain the wages of labor and the earnings of capital as the vampire bat is said to suck the lifeblood of its victim. Nearly all of these taxes are ultimately paid by that indefinable being, the consumer; and he pays them in a way which does not call his attention to the fact that he is paying a tax—pays them in such small amounts and in such insidious modes that he does not notice it, and is not likely to take the trouble to remonstrate effectually. Those who pay the money directly to the tax collector are not only not interested in opposing a tax which

> they so easily shift from their own shoulders, but are very frequently interested in its imposition and maintenance, as are other powerful interests which profit, or expect to profit, by the increase of prices which such taxes bring about. (George [1879] 1912, Book VIII, ch. 4)

In New South Wales and the other colonies of Australia, where much acreage was held by the wealthy, the idea of implementing George's single tax became briefly attractive in the years 1890–1898 as a solution to the monopolization of private land, although the remedy did not fit well with socialist notions of the state instead taking over all the property; however, some thinkers, including Rose Summerfield, were able to advocate both positions at the same time (Scates 1986, 72, 73). Unfortunately, as Scates notes, neither the ASL nor the STL ultimately produced reforms that would have fundamentally benefited the ordinary people for whom they campaigned:

> Like the socialist, the Single Taxer had no place in a party prepared to barter principle for electoral success. Their debacle was symptomatic of the failure of nineteenth-century radicalism as a whole. (Scates 1986, 94)

In December 1892, the ASL held a conference at Leigh House, with delegates coming from affiliates across New South Wales and Victoria. It featured an ambitious agenda for discussion, including a proposal to turn the organization into a political party that would develop an election platform, and a number of progressive ideas, including nationalization of land and of banks, removal of the property ownership qualification for jury service, universal adult suffrage, and proportional representation. But despite the many radical proposals, the Australian Labor Party that developed alongside and contemporaneously with these proposals was far less committed to reform, and its rejection of a nationalization proposal in 1897 led to a formal split the next year from the ASL, which kept to a more socialist agenda (McIlroy 2003, 12; "Socialist Conference" 1892; "The Socialist Conference" 1892).

ILLEGITIMACY

Rose Summerfield was both a women's rights activist and a freethinking critic of Christian practices, so it is no surprise that she decries the scourge of labeling children and adults alike as being "illegitimate," since that convention, it can be argued, represents both an insult to women and an inappropriate effort by outsiders to control their behavior, often as an attempt to inflict one's religious doctrine onto others. Why, Rose asks, do we perpetuate this practice of shaming the innocent victim of the disapproved behavior, the child? She begins her poem, "Branded Children" with a quotation from Shakespeare's *King Lear*, in which Edmund, the illegitimate son of the Earl of Gloucester, rages against the negative consequences of his birth, asking why his legitimate brother, Edgar, is entitled to inherit their father's property, rendering himself a casualty of unnatural, human-made prejudice and law (*King Lear* 1.2.5–9; Summerfield 1898c). Centuries later, in the Australia of 1898, this cruel tradition persists:

> They are branded children, so the law proclaims;
> Often love-sweet children, with no fathers' names. (Summerfield 1898c)

As was routine for Summerfield, she identifies here another urgent need for social change. Like the voice of Shakespeare speaking through the character of Edmund, Rose recognizes the unfair, unnatural role of illegitimacy in society, and like the American feminist, Tennie C. Claflin (later known as Lady Cook), she is also aware how its usage benefits men (Claflin 1898, 81–82, 1922, 12–13; Shone 2019, 150–151):

> Let no creature languish thro' another's fall,
> For a mother's anguish is the worst of all.
> Why should we uphold it shame of old-time days?
> Hasten to unfold it, our-time better ways;
> Let us strive to alter laws that keep men poor;
> Let us never falter while these wrongs endure. (Summerfield 1898c)

However, with respect to the need to ameliorate this infliction of human indignity, not all Sydney-area radicals were in agreement. Responding to Summerfield's poem, Carlotta, who at that point was editing the "Woman Items" column in the Wagga, NSW *Worker* in which the verses had appeared, cautioned that "[c]hildren must suffer for the sins of their parents, and the sooner parents realize this the better" (Carlotta 1898b). Warning that relaxing the humiliation attendant on giving birth to an illegitimate child would "be an encouragement to vice," Carlotta (1898b) insisted that the only appropriate solution to the problem would be for the man and woman in question to marry.

Replying to Carlotta in the subsequent issue, Rose Summerfield, denying that her goal was to encourage vice, cautioned that "facts and not theories have to be faced," urging her critic to view the problem as an economic issue, rather than as a moral one. Because of the need to work to survive, people move around and are often unable to settle down, but a consequence of this should not mean that the more disadvantaged residents of New South Wales should be forced to abandon hope of obtaining love and affection or not in any way be able to act upon their natural drives (1898d).

> [W]e find that numbers of young men and women who honestly love each other, but who perhaps are helping to support parents and keep a home going, cannot get their parents' consent to their marriage; hence trouble ensues. Where no sin was intended misery steps in. (Summerfield 1898d)

In a rejoinder to Summerfield published in a later *Worker* issue, Carlotta reemphasized the morality perspective in a characteristically Victorian way that offered even less hope for those deemed illegitimate:

> Suppose young people cannot get their parents' consent; suppose they cannot afford to marry; if love is love, and, no girl can learn this too soon, it can wait, and be the better for the waiting. Self-control is a part of love, and if young people can not afford to marry, one would think they could still less afford to act thoughtlessly and selfishly. (Carlotta 1898a)

In the same column, a contributor who signed herself "A Badd Lott" expressed support for the ideas presented in Summerfield's poem, and perhaps carried them further along a line trodden by other feminist thinkers, including Claflin, who, like Summerfield, compared marriage to prostitution, questioning the use of terms like vice and illegitimacy to impart control over women's lives.

> Hats are raised and heads bowed to the woman who sells herself into wealthy but loveless matrimony, whilst we draw our draperies aside and harden our hearts and faces in rigid righteousness when one who has "loved not wisely, but too well" passes, especially if she is brave and motherly (we call it brazen) enough to have her child in her arms; and as to her child, I have always been too dense to understand why it should be "branded." My eyes and ears assure me that such little ones are as sound, morally and physically, as those born in wedlock. (A Badd Lott 1898)

Chapter 4

A Major Thinker, Mischaracterized and Misunderstood

RACE AND CHEAP LABOR

Mark Hearn (2004, 71–72) designates Rose a racist for her argument in her "Master and Man" speech that, in order to maintain their profit margins, capitalists will import "slaves" from other parts of the world who will then work for lower wages; he notes that she mentions the squalor in which some Chinese immigrants to Australia are living in one area of Sydney:

> Assigning prejudicial meanings to the body of the Other—the smell, filth, leering faces of these aliens huddled like beasts—provided Summerfield's audience with a powerfully visceral production of their shared and fearful loathing. (Hearn 2004, 72)

But is this fundamentally an example of prejudice, rather than unacquaintedness and mere criticism, given that the Chinese and the others that she mentions here, Italians, Syrians, and Indians, are all living outside the social milieu and acting in uncommon ways? She does refer to Chinese people as being "almond-eyed" (Hearn 2000, 71; Summerfield 1892b, 6), but while, today, we would probably feel that the focus on a group's physical characteristics automatically renders it an unfortunate comment, it is also an approximate statement of fact. When people are unfamiliar with the lives of strangers, except mainly in the context of the red light district where the principal interaction between them and you so far has been one that you, Rose, view as including them having made sexist comments about you—apparently, some faces did leer—the offenders may not necessarily be accorded the benefit of the doubt. Elsewhere, arguing in favor of the vote for women, she writes:

> [I]f the women are to be excluded it means that the bearers and teachers, the guides and helpers of men are to be fixed on a lower plane than the ignorant

> aboriginals and the drunken wastrels of society. Surely there is something lacking in the State that permits this. (Summerfield 1898a)

Here Aborigines (a term today often considered an inaccurate and unsuitable name for the original residents) are criticized as a group, but not because of their ethnic characteristics. Rather, building on some indigenous Australian problems with alcohol and the prohibitions that were used to prevent them from purchasing it, Rose associates them unfairly here with drunks and other ne'er-do-wells, as people who fail to behave appropriately. This much resembles important United States feminist Elizabeth Cady Stanton's use of "Sambo," an offensive term applied to black people, which has led to Cady Stanton being arbitrarily deemed a racist, for example, by Davis (2008, 145, 210). When she used the term, Cady Stanton was not seeking to demean black people or deny them the vote, but arguing in the currently accepted vernacular that it would be unfair if women, who already enjoyed equal rights and responsibility in some areas of social life, should have to wait to be enfranchised until after black men were given this empowerment (Stanton 1868, 373). Similarly, Summerfield asks why all women, notwithstanding their own levels of sophistication, morality, and conscientiousness, must stand in line behind every male, even the most reproachable, and receive the vote last, a success which so far had not been accomplished.

For Summerfield, it is the role played by outsiders that is important, not their race, not their racial features, but the way they have been and may to a greater extent in the near future be used by employers to undermine workers, their pay, and their ensuing standard of living. In "Master and Man," she also demonstrates her concern about the conditions faced by these Others, those better able to be exploited:

> They dare not ravish your women and girls; they dare not force you to work until you drop, like they can force the poor Kanaka. You have more manhood, more courage than the poor unfortunate black who is torn from his island home and kindred, and forced into a miserable subjection. (Summerfield 1892b, 6)

Moreover, she is speaking and writing in the nineteenth century: people are less familiar with social difference; the world in general is a less comfortable, less tolerant place. Summerfield's argument is in general the ASL and labor union perspective, an economic one that recognizes a questionable role for some outsiders in the economy. Of course, it is regrettable that this position bestows on its advocate a superficially racially-conscious association and, as noted below, the local anarchists at that time had a far better approach to dealing with the underlying problem, but Rose is not a racist in any meaningful way.

When Summerfield writes elsewhere about Chinese immigrants as follows, "But you must come with me all round—in Goulburn-street, with its vile smells and dirty rookeries. There is the big fat oily Chinese, whose eyes follow you like glittering snake's eyes, and other cadaverous opium-sotted Celestials who chill you as they pass" (Summerfield 1895b), her position is undergirded by lack of familiarity with different cultures and racial features which is typical of the age, but some of the dismay lies in recognition of the nearby presence of an opium den when the smoking of opium is inconsistent with the ideals of the majority. In her Gundagai speech, later in the year, she asks:

> If your Government were what it ought to be. . . . The alien Mongol, the Chinese with their leprosy-breeding vegetables, their unnaturally diseased forced salads, their vile opium dens, where so many of our sisters go to destruction—would not be wanted, would not be kept, and am I not right in saying it would not be allowed. ("The Workers Union of N.S.W." 1892)

When she asks in "Master and Man," "'Work early and late every day in the week like them for a small wage, huddled up together ten in a room'; were you willing to live like 'the waste of Italy's fair shores'?" (Hearn 2004, 71; Summerfield 1892b, 6), is this not a sensible reaction for the mainstream Australian who wishes not to have to compete with cheaper outside labor, albeit a response that might have been phrased with greater sensitivity? But the real object of Summerfield's ire is surely the circumstances under which some immigrants live and are obliged to tolerate, and the threat that this poses to the standard of living of the majority community. Part of the reason she worked to establish cooperative laundries in Sydney and Bourke, NSW, was to put an end to the hard, sweated labor of Chinese laundry workers ("Australian Workers: New Labour Organisation" 1892; Spence 1893; Summerfield 1898q). At its heart, this is an economic argument, not a bigoted one. When she speaks of "wiping out the colored curse, who do so much damage to the furniture trade, the hawking and laundry industry, and make it almost impossible for the average Australian to compete with them in market gardening" (Summerfield 1893b), she is concerned about the undermining of the wages of Australian labor, including its women. Again, this is an ill-chosen phrase, of which few people would approve today, but it is not an anachronistic show of support for Hitler. She is actually opposed to all forms of slavery, including wage slavery. Like labor activists all over the world and in other eras, she sees how capitalists will lower salary costs to achieve higher profits. This is how capitalism works. As she notes, "It is the same system that produces the tyrant employer and the homeless wanderer" ("The Workers Union of N.S.W." 1892). Have real wages not fallen in the developed world over the decades since, due to globalized competition, for example, from workers in China who are denied many of their basic rights? Is it racism to want workers in more developed countries, who maintain some protection of their liberties and standard of living, to be able to continue to compete with those in China who are being cruelly exploited?

Harvey (2010, 302) notes that "Rose claimed in Sydney's *Worker* magazine that 'as a race surely we are demoralized enough without mixing with an inferior one.'" However, in the article in question, titled "Stray Notes," where she comes to that unjustifiable conclusion, criticizing Chinese, Arab, and Indian people in an unfair way that is certainly no longer appropriate, the specific objects of her denunciation who inspire her ire are men standing out in the street leering, a cook whom she saw spit into the meal he was preparing, and hawkers she believes are selling drugs. Despite the ultimate lack of soundness to her argument, it is not their race that she faults, but what she believes to be the content of their character (Summerfield 1898k). Ironically, Hearn and Knowles ask:

> The biographer must conduct a sympathetic interrogation. . . . Why did she express disgust at non-Europeans? What do these attitudes reveal about how Summerfield felt about herself? These are difficult questions that cannot always be answered; the biographer must ask them, although not to crudely label or judge the historical subject: empathy requires recognition of all the aspects of personality, behaviour and belief that may be uncovered from the evidence, and a willingness to face the complex and at times contradictory meanings that flow from a life and its clamorous, demanding context. (Hearn and Knowles 2004, 2)

Analysis sympathetic to the life and thought of Rose Summerfield, a refusal to "crudely label or judge the historical subject," should perhaps reject the opinion that her "disgust" was applied to "non-Europeans." Rather, time and time again, she applied it much more specifically to those behaviors and circumstances about which she felt dismay or concern.

At an ASL meeting at Leigh House on May 29, 1892, Rose provided entertainment to begin a meeting that protested the possibility of introducing contract labor of "black" workers, Kanakas from New Caledonia, into Australasia in general and Queensland's sugar industry in particular. Within a decade, a few thousand sugar cane-producing Kanakas would be expelled as pressure for a "White Australia" grew (Iacovetta, Quinlan, and Radforth 1996, 96–97; Lake and Reynolds 2008, 137). From the ASL perspective, such a supply of extra labor was viewed as yet something else planned by the monopolists who controlled many aspects of production, and which would further undermine the conditions and goals of the labor force as a whole. During the meeting, a participant called A. Thomsen clarified the position in a way that is not so much xenophobic as an example of realistic common sense about how the economy works: a reporter summarized his perspective as follows: "As socialists they recognised the black man as a brother, but it was cruelty to force him from his home on the Islands to compete with men who had attained a higher standard of living" ("Black Labor" 1892). With similar care, the gathering passed a resolution: "That this meeting emphatically protests against the introduction of colored labor under the contract system, inasmuch as it is inimical to the interests of the white population" ("Black Labor" 1892). Opposition to importation of cheaper labor by union activists and those who speak for them, especially when the contracts in question restrict the rights and opportunities of those being brought into a country, has long been widespread and should not be routinely attributed to racism. Some of Summerfield's concerns about minorities from Asia and Southern Europe were likewise prompted by her dislike of the red light area, what she saw as its immoral atmosphere, and the presence of drugs and prostitution there. Hearn (2004, 72) notes that "Rae Frances refers to the fear of miscegenation between Asian men and white women that gripped the late colonial imagination," an occurrence that would mostly have annoyed white men, but Rose, who was a woman, has nothing to say about miscegenation—just about the danger of the people who currently exploit Australian workers finding someone else who will toil for even less so that more profit can be made, much as contemporary large-scale businesses have moved from the developed world to China, Vietnam, the Philippines, Haiti, and Mexico.

In her "Master and Man" performance, Summerfield also criticizes the breaks that are given to investors such as George and William Chaffey, who in 1887 were allowed by the colony of Victoria, following a drought, to purchase 250,000 acres of land near Mildura, on the Murray River, and who turned this opportunity into a vast profit, selling small parcels of the property to settlers for at least 20 times what they had paid. She criticizes not only the fact that this land has been transferred from public to private ownership, but that the development makes land much more expensive for others to use ("Smoke Ho!" 1893b; Summerfield 1892b, 7–8). Here, her argument is again about outsiders prospering at the expense of Australians, not that people like the Chaffey brothers, from North America, are racially inferior:

> If your Government treat you like this, what will you do about it? Let strangers come in and get your land for a trifle, make fortunes on it, and in most cases go home again to spend it. . . . Your Governments are very favorable to them; they like to see them coming; they welcome them. They would try and educate you in the belief that these are the proper people, the very ones, mind you, who are wanted amongst us. But are they? (Summerfield 1892b, 8)

In addition to her concerns about the direction the economy is taking, Rose voices a moralistic concern about decay in the social environment, regardless of the ethnicity of those who participate:

> White and black and yellow scum huddled and banded together, steeped themselves in opium and poison drinks, that for a while blunted their misery, and while this inferno is sucking in new victims a bell peals forth its sweet chimes, the fœtid air of this slum mars not the liquid notes. What is the strain? Hark! how it floats over these haunts of crime and loathesomeness [*sic*]. Oh! the mockery of it, the cant—"The earth is the Lord's and the fullness thereof." (Summerfield 1896d)

Elsewhere, Hearn (2000, 376–377) writes that "In William Lane's colony Cadogan [Rose] found the same insidious multiculturalism that had weakened her faith in Australia." However, it was not multiculturalism that she objected to, since multiculturalism did not yet exist. The immigrants she described were not well integrated into, or generally seen as being a part of, the Sydney community. What did exist was an unfortunate subclass of persons who were due to their circumstances easily exploitable; she did not want other, marginally better off workers to be undermined by cheaper labor. Hearn continues:

> The ingrained fears that fed Rose Cadogan's racism led her from Australia and into despair, realising too late that she could not get back. Nor could she conceive of how to live amongst strangers. (Hearn 2000, 376–377)

Although it is true that Rose wished to return to Australia and was unable to do this, she and her second husband, Jack Cadogan, moved away from the Cosme colony into mainstream Paraguayan society where they operated a store, and attempted to reduce the incidence of malaria and hookworm on the part of their neighbors, from whom they received encouragement and to whom they dispensed their medical knowledge ("Death of Rose Summerfield" 1922; Souter [1968] 2012, 289). Summerfield's later life in Paraguay, and the activities of one of her sons, León, on behalf of the indigenous people there, which Hearn acknowledges, bear testimony to a very different Rose, who participated benevolently in the life of the whole South American community.

Of course, a better solution to the presence of minority workers than that sought by Rose and her union colleagues had already been suggested in an editorial in *Honesty*, the journal of the Melbourne Anarchist Club (MAC), which pointed out:

> [T]here are not fifty thousand Chinese in the whole of Australasia, as against two million eight hundred thousand Europeans,—sixty-five of us to every

> Chinaman. Think of it: sixty-five white men afraid to compete with one yellow skin! ("Chinese Labor" 1887, 37)

Indeed, the solution suggested in the editorial seems to be very much in accordance with the economic reforms that Summerfield was advocating:

> The fact is that statute law has monopolised the wealth of nature in the hands of a few idlers; and the workers—Chinese and European—are cutting each other's throat for the crumbs from the rich man's table, when they might more advantageously cease piling the fruits of their labor upon that table. The Chinese, like ourselves, are the victims of monopoly and exploitation. ("Chinese Labor" 1887, 37)

This *Honesty* article, treating Chinese immigrants as equals and equal victims as it does, is also more reasonable than the views of Summerfield's erstwhile secularist colleague, Joseph Symes, from whose intellectual leadership members of the MAC had diverged; when running for office on behalf of the Freethought Party, Symes suggested the best solution was to avoid all contact with people of Chinese origin ("Mr. Joseph Symes" 1889).

Nothing in Hearn's analysis, or indeed in the whole "Master and Man" speech, or in anything else that Summerfield said or wrote that still survives, justifies his conclusion that:

> Rose drew a potent lesson from the symbolic environment that she shared with her fellow workers and radicals and constructed a fable that could galvanise them into action—a spur to their freedom at the expense of significant others barely present in numbers, but sufficient for the purposes of totemic vilification. (Hearn 2004, 72)

Rather, the fable lies in obsessively applying twenty-first-century dogmas to the nineteenth century as if people back then should have automatically behaved exactly in the same way as, many decades later, and following many long excruciating battles to achieve social progress, we now realize is a better approach, or, alternatively, in accordance with an ideological slant to which we personally, but not they, have decided to commit ourselves. The Melbourne anarchists, to their credit, were ahead of the curve in this respect, but it does not follow that Summerfield and her labor activist colleagues were wrong to sense the looming danger to their livelihoods at the time when the excesses of capitalism observed few boundaries.

On November 23, 1901, the writer of a column in the Sydney-area *Worker* called "The Grafter's Wallet" reported the receipt of a letter from Rose, now living in Paraguay, in which it said she had commented:

> It is a fine country, but, owing to the ignorance, indolence, and superstition of the natives, it is a poor place to live in, and anyone may do better in any part of Australia. One regrets that such good workers in the reform cause should be buried among strangers and retrogrades. ("The Grafter's Wallet" 1901)

In the original, no quotation marks are given, and it is not clear whether (1) the passage comes directly from Summerfield's letter, or (2) whether its editor is paraphrasing what is reported as having been written "lengthily" (1901), or (3) whether the editor is editorializing and giving a generalized summation of themes to be found in what Rose actually wrote. Unfortunately, both Hearn in two places (2000, 377, 2004, 79) and Harvey (2010, 302) present the passage from the *Worker* as a quotation, as though the question about its precise nature had been automatically resolved, there being no doubt that Summerfield actually wrote these words. The questionable quotation is then used by Harvey to justify the conclusion that "[i]n particular, Rose struggled to relate to the native Guarani Indians" (302), which, in the light of the medical services she chose to provide to her native neighbors, a fact that Harvey concedes, seems unlikely.

RESEARCH AND OPEN-MINDEDNESS

Hearn's (2004, 72) reference to the work of Rae Frances and others, with their attempts to reformulate the history of Australia in terms of its persistent (and continuing) racism, identifies scholarship that is appropriate and accurate, and many of the examples they discuss are horrible to recall, but Frances's research does not necessarily support the more extreme thesis that racism is the independent variable that accounts for all social change. She writes:

> Initially, maintaining a particular class hierarchy and heterosexual norm assumed primacy over any considerations of racial hierarchies. Official priorities, however, were quickly modified in the light of popular attitudes and colonial realities. As white society achieved supremacy over the indigenous population, and non-white labourers were imported, particularly in the north, the preservation of white supremacy ensured that racial considerations became a major issue for colonial governments and important pressure groups within white colonial society. However, the very fact that racial *hierarchies* were an issue meant that questions of class and status were inextricably linked. (Frances 1999, 121)

Neither does the case of Rose Summerfield fit well under such an ambit. For instance, Lake and Reynolds (2008, 44–45) note the racist character of some of James Bryce's ideas as expressed in his influential book *The American*

Commonwealth (1888) and in an article called "Thoughts on the Negro Problem," which appeared in the *North American Review* in 1891, in which Bryce considered whether Americans of African origin, being "an alien element, unabsorbed and unabsorbable" should be deported to somewhere else. He argued that it had been wrong to give black people the vote:

> Emancipation found them [black Americans] utterly ignorant; and the grant of the suffrage found them as unfit for political rights as any population could be. (Bryce 1888, 92; Lake and Reynolds 2008, 49)

Similarly, his colleague, Charles Pearson, the author of another significant work, *National Life and Character: A Forecast* (1893) and a Liberal politician from Victoria who had first met Bryce at Oxford University, applied the argument in a ridiculously exaggerated way to the presence of non-white persons in Australia:

> We know that coloured and white labour cannot exist side by side; we are well aware that China can swamp us with a single year's surplus population; and we know that if national existence is sacrificed to the working of a few mines and sugar plantations, it is not the Englishman in Australia alone, but the whole civilised world that will be the losers. (Lake and Reynolds 2008, 77; Pearson 1893, 16)

However, these extremist views, which powerfully influenced the development of a White Australia policy (which, with the support of the AWU, would continue until Gough Whitlam became prime minister in 1972), enshrined in the Immigration Restriction Act of 1901 and the Pacific Island Labourers Act of the same year, were not shared by Rose Summerfield, who from 1899 onward lived in Paraguay, and who was claiming only that, since indigenous men were enfranchised (in New South Wales and some other colonies/states until 1902), so women should also be, and that the standard of living of workers in Australia should not be further undermined by competition from people apt to tolerate even worse conditions ("AWU Timeline" 2020; Harvey 2010, 304; Lake and Reynolds 2008, 150, 155; Levey 2019, 84, 85). In the same measured way, making a similar argument in the United States about voting later exaggerated by modern critics, Elizabeth Cady Stanton wrote:

> If this nation is not ready to admit its virtuous, educated, tax-paying women to the polls, then we say the fewer men the better. . . . But when Mr. Pomeroy [the editor of the *La Crosse Democrat* newspaper in Wisconsin] says that black men are not as well qualified to make laws as white men, we cannot agree with him. (Stanton 1868, 373)

The implication that Summerfield or Cady Stanton were saying much more than they actually said is to distort the words and lives of two tremendously important feminist thinkers. Unfortunately, with respect to its immigration policies today, Australia, which violates international law by denying access to asylum seekers if they arrive by boat, imprisoning some of them for years in detention centers in Papua New Guinea or Nauru, appears to have retained some of its prior attitudes (Albeck-Ripka and Mzezewa 2021; Doherty 2016). Nevertheless, it would not be appropriate to criticize all Australians for the existence of this aberrant practice, or to blame its occurrence on every Australian who favors having some immigration control. In the same way, notwithstanding the categorization of the White Australia policy in 1906 by Australian Prime Minister Alfred Deakin in terms of a battle between civilized and noncivilized races, appalling as that was, there is no evidence that Summerfield, living in Paraguay, was aware of it or endorsed it (Boncardo 2008, 30; Lake and Reynolds 2008, 9).

Moreover, even though Summerfield had rather more contact with William Lane, and initially lived in the Cosme settlement from which the latter had recently departed for New Zealand, and even though Lane had insisted that the New Australia projects be restricted to white people, giving the same racist rationalization as Deakin that separation would preserve civilization, nothing like the same tenacity or all-encompassing philosophy can be observed in any of the extant writings of, or reports about, the activities of Rose Summerfield, who essentially just wanted to make it possible for working families to live on the income they made from their hard work and have a decent place to live where women would be treated with respect. Lane outlined his fear of racial minorities when he published *White or Yellow? A Story of Race War in A.D. 1908* in the weekly newspaper, the *Boomerang*, but Summerfield did not write anything of that nature, and it is wrong to represent her ideas as if she did (Hannan 1966, 10, 85; Perez 2016, 165; Thompson 2013).

This argument about how best to explain aspects of Australian and other colonial history has long been the subject of debate. For example, Andrew Markus comments:

> The explanation for the treatment of non-European immigrants in nineteenth century Australia has been the subject of historical controversy since the mid-1950s. . . . Most recently there have been attempts to demonstrate the precise inter-relationship of various factors, with several historians arguing that pre-existing racism must be the starting point in any explanation. The most forceful exponent of such an interpretation is Verity Burgmann. (Markus 1985, 86)

For Markus, Burgmann's approach, and that of others of similar views, is problematic:

> Burgmann underestimates the significance of shifts in racial (and ethnocentric) thought within society and across time; indeed, development of ideas is rarely noted. . . . By what criteria do we plot with precision the establishment, shifting nature and demise of such ideas? It is obvious that problems surround the precise delineation of ideas at such a level of generality. (Markus 1985, 87)

In response, Burgmann describes Markus's methodological approach as being "baloney." She writes:

> Personally, I am still inclined to the view that Australian racism was not created by the restrictive trade practices of the nineteenth century working class. Such an explanation for racism cannot explain middle-class racism, as it is implausible that middle-class people would become racially motivated out of concern for working-class wages and conditions. Of course, inability to explain middle-class racism does not perturb proponents of the baloney view, as racism to them is largely or entirely the prerogative of the worker. They prefer to ignore the evidence that racism pre-existed the organisation of Australian workers and was present at all levels in society, amongst all classes of people. The belief on the part of the labour movement that non-white immigrants would willingly work for poor wages in bad conditions was not a cause of racism, as Markus would have us believe, but an effect of the racism already prevalent. (Burgmann 1985b, 98–99)

She continues that "Markus explains the hostility to the Chinese . . . in terms of what the Chinese did or did not do, a method of analysis which . . . shares the assumptions of the prejudiced that it is the behaviour of the immigrants that is responsible for the hostility of the host population towards them" (Burgmann 1985b, 100).

Rose Summerfield's perspective is similarly framed in terms of behavior, but it is not racist in a substantive way. She argues that the employment of lower-paid, more exploitable groups undermines the economic position of the majority; the behavior of those minorities is unavoidable and unintentional, but it is nevertheless behavior. Similarly, she criticizes people who smoke opium, live in squalor, and sexually harass women; this is also behavior, but not necessarily unintentional. As Markus points out, dogmatically rejecting alternative theories by insisting on the primacy of racism as a causal factor is to explain social history through the lens of a dominant ideology. Thus, when Burgmann rejects "uncritical acceptance of arguments advanced by the opponents of the Chinese which leads to a blaming of the victims of prejudice for the prejudice manifested towards them" (Markus 1985, 86), she imposes "a deterministic straightjacket" (88) on the research of others. Moreover, since other destitute immigrants were often targeted for criticism, even those who shared the same racial category as the Australian majority, there must be something wrong with prioritization of the question in terms of ethnicity (89–90):

> Yet if any group (not only non Europeans, but the Irish and even the 'kith and kin' of the British colonists) can become the target for racism, irrespective of appearance or cultural background, racist ideology can hardly provide a sufficient explanation for the definition of outgroups. (Markus 1985, 90)

In similar fashion, Gareth Stedman Jones's groundbreaking work, *Languages of Class: Studies in English Working Class History 1832–1982* (Jones 1983), has questioned the fact that "much current social and labour history writing has been informed by Marxist assumptions or questions" (1983, 3), leading to erroneous conclusions, and for example, distorting the manner in which the Chartism of the 1830s and 1840s was in the past portrayed, since some of its details did not fit well with preordained dogmas concerning class. Unfortunately, many of the arguments and accomplishments of Chartist activists were transmuted, watered down, or ignored, while scholars intentionally or unintentionally wrote about Chartism as a means of promoting Marxist doctrine (Epstein 1985, 74–75, 1986, 195; Gray 1986, 368). As Bongiorno (1994, 14–16) notes in his study of labor politics in Victoria from 1890 to 1914, although many radical historians have "accepted the primacy of economic class as a tool of historical explanation, . . . their treatment of the concept was inchoate. The standard explanation of the emergence of the Labor Party was that it was the outcome of increasing class consciousness, manifested in the emergence of the 'new unionism' of shearers and miners." Instead, Bongiorno, like Stedman Jones, emphasizes that class is a complex phenomenon, and a "contested concept" (16). Perhaps, therefore, the best advice available for researchers is to realize that not every element of labor history should be assumed *a priori* to have been caused by a particular variable such as class or race, but should instead be investigated in more penetrating detail. Both class and race are wide-ranging notions, frequently customized to a project unintentionally due to ideological commitment, and anyway both controversial and difficult to define, and use of them to explicate human phenomena will perforce open a study to criticism, while attempts to formally operationalize them to ascertain causes and associations as part of a quasi-empirical approach will of necessity oversimplify their denotation and greatly increase the potential for error.

In Australia, of course, Chartism mapped out its own history, partly because the land issue so dear to Summerfield's heart was central to Chartist concerns, and also because that viewpoint had extended via immigration of its advocates to the Ballarat goldfields area in Victoria where, about a decade later Rose would be born (McIlroy 2003, 6–9). As Lloyd Churchward described:

> In Australia [as opposed to England], Chartist ideas had a much broader support, drawing in middle-class as well as working-class elements of the population. This was because the main political struggle in Australia after 1842 (and especially after 1850) united workers and middle classes against the landowning squattocracy. (Churchward, quoted in McIlroy 2003, 5)

Excessive concentration by researchers on the explanatory power of class has led to misunderstandings of the nature of Chartism. Similarly, Elizabeth Cady Stanton was maybe the most important American feminist thinker, but the inaccurate attribution to her of racism (along with attempts to suppress her in fact thoughtful, original, and erudite criticism of Christianity) has caused much of her significance to be obscured from contemporary view. In the same way, designating Summerfield as a racist is potentially to obliterate a source of much neglected, albeit somewhat obscured intellectual content to be found among her biographical accomplishments, an erasure that it is, of course, the objective of the current work to rectify.

Chapter 5

Settler in Paraguay

LEAVING AUSTRALIA

On March 28, 1899, a party was held at the ASL's Mayfield Hall on Castlereagh Street in Sydney to say good-bye to Rose and husband Jack, who were scheduled to depart for Paraguay on April 5. Friends and colleagues gathered together to thank Rose for thirteen years of service to radical causes. Master of ceremonies, George Black, said that "he did not doubt that wherever she went her good work would be continued" ("Social to Mrs. Cadogan" 1899). W. G. Spence, now a Labor member of parliament, was another attendee (Hearn 2000, 376–377, 2004, 78–79; "Social to Mrs. Cadogan" 1899). About a month earlier, she had given a lecture at the same location with the title, "Flowers and their Suggestions." Referencing the transcendentalist visions of Walt Whitman, Henry David Thoreau, and Ralph Waldo Emerson as being prompted by appreciation of the open air, Rose pointed out that if flowers are allowed appropriate access to resources and are treated with care, their own self-reliance will allow them to thrive without any need to be controlled, thereby in their freedom creating beauty for the benefit of humans. Men and women in the Australian colonies, on the other hand, have organized their economic system less fruitfully by denying most people access to land, and thus many of the poor find their lives are a struggle to survive, an unnecessarily ugly predicament. In addition to this creative exposition of one of her key issues, the need for restructuring of land ownership, Summerfield also made reference to her distrust of religious thinking, noting that "[i]f we worshipped more at Flora's shrine it would undoubtedly be to our advantage, as we should learn to look more for the joys right here, and less for imagining joys to come" ("Lecture: Mrs. Cadogan on 'Flowers'" 1899). Perhaps contemplating also her imminent departure for the challenges of a future life in a barely built farming settlement, she said, "And now I know the making of the best persons; it is to live in the open air, and eat and sleep with the earth" ("Lecture: Mrs. Cadogan on 'Flowers'" 1899).

For Summerfield, the attraction of land, which many of the poorer residents of Sydney, living in slums, had no hope of ever owning and working for their personal benefit, derived also from recognition of the underlying economics. The *Shearers' and General Laborers' Record*, for whom she wrote some material during 1893, included a paragraph written by prominent anarchist Peter Kropotkin that urged Britain to increase its cultivation of wheat and other agricultural products in order to lessen hunger and make more food available adjacent to the cities where people lived ("The Productive Property of Land" 1893). Whether or not Rose was involved in the editorial decision to include the excerpt is unknown, but Kropotkin's logic was shared by her and the other union activists with whom she worked. The passage quoted in the paper, which was not cited, was taken from Kropotkin's "The Coming Reign of Plenty," which appeared in the June 1888 edition of *Nineteenth Century*; the article was later incorporated into Kropotkin's ([1899] 1912) book *Fields, Factories and Workshops*. In 1907, when Ernie Lane, who had been inspired by Kropotkin's writings and by the example of how he lived his life, now returning to Australia after leaving Colonia Cosme, and traveling via London, had an opportunity to meet in person one of his erstwhile heroes, he found the Russian to be not as he had imagined, for Kropotkin was convinced of the dangers, rather than of any appeal, of centralized socialism. For Ernie, this incompatibility with communism was seen as a defect of anarchist theory (Lane [1939] 1993, 96–98), though once Kropotkin moved back home in 1917, he quickly found evidence in Lenin's behavior that his suspicions had been far from defective, suggesting that Lane's dismissal of his "perverse adherence to anarchial dogma" (98) was rather inapt.

Rose believed that human life was improvable if not perfectible, that good deeds should be actively pursued, and that eventually human beings would enjoy much better conditions and opportunities than those she had encountered in Australia. This caused her to embrace the search for workable acreage in South America that could be farmed and organized in a communitarian fashion. In her poem, "There's Always Good in Work" (Summerfield 1898o), she urges others to reject "self-love," anticipating a time when the disadvantaged will be able to rise above their circumstances and achieve revolutionary change:

> And some day will arise, a pow'r compact,
> To mould a fairer path for men to tread;
> With life's delights for all who care to woo. (Summerfield 1898o)

She went to Paraguay believing her life from that point on would be much improved but, unfortunately, the initial settlement project, New Australia, had already self-destructed due to the failure of its participants' efforts, and in particular those of its leader, William Lane who, like Lenin, was unable to work cooperatively, to give and take; the vision she held, even before she sailed, was already wrecked, a disappointing disaster. The reality was much less achievable than what she had hoped for in her poem, where she exhorted others to try and rectify the problems she saw around her:

> Then see to it—let not thy lamp burn low,
> Its glow all gone ere you essay the task;
> Forth in thy manhood's lustre bravely go;
> And from one beacon false remove the mask.
> Or lead sweet pity forth where women weep,
> Or where frail children battle with disease;
> Or grim want doth its fearful orgie keep;
> Do but one kindly deed a pang to ease. (Summerfield 1898o)

In another poem, "Sympathy" (Summerfield 1898l), Rose had evoked the power of mutual feeling and mutual aid to bring about cooperation between people, but on the first voyage of the *Royal Tar*, taking the initial wave of settlers to Paraguay, competing interests and attempts by factions to impose rules on other people had already effectively destroyed the enterprise:

> Tyrants tremble 'neath its sway, at its growing power to-day.
> It will usher in the birth of the reign of peace on earth;
> Sympathy will yet be found round the nations firmly bound—
> Welding them in brotherhood as no other power could.
> Sympathy speed on apace, stamp on all thy kindly trace,
> Till all men and women know—all can reap the good they sow.
> (Summerfield 1898l)

In Paraguay, unfortunately, William Lane, capitalizing on the charitable fellow-feeling of many of those who joined him in the first few weeks of the initial settlement, commenced to impose a tyranny of his own making.

FAR FROM PARADISE

From a modern perspective, Paraguay seems an unlikely place to construct an idealistic workers' commune. Graham Greene's books *Travels with My Aunt* and *The Honorary Consul* have contained particularly negative portrayals of life in that nation. These works are fictional, but like all of his creations, the stories they tell were based on well-researched reality. Benz describes Greene's journalistic work as follows, in a way that has relevance also to his novels:

> The concreteness of Greene's prose is meant to give readers the experience of having been somewhere, of having seen and felt a certain place at a certain time, unencumbered by cliches and slogans. (Benz 1998, 10)

In *The Honorary Consul*, Charley Fortnum, the British government's representative in a town just across the river from Paraguay in Argentina, is kidnapped by former political prisoners opposed to the actual brutal dictatorship of "the General," Alfredo Stroessner, the opponent of communism who ruled Paraguay from 1954 to 1989, a place where critics languished in cells spread out among local police stations to keep them from communicating with each other, and even the topics of priests' sermons were monitored by law enforcement and could be proscribed (see, for example, Saguier 1979). In Paraguay, "[t]he Jesuits do as they can. But they are watched by the police. Their telephones are tapped. If anyone seems dangerous he is quickly pushed across the river. They do not kill him. The Yankees would not like a priest to be killed" (Greene 1973, 141). And perhaps this is why Catholic Church leaders coexist with such a terrible dictator, a situation that Benz (2003, 117) argues may for Greene be preferable to endorsing the violence of the kidnappers in the novel, one of whom is a former priest. In *The Honorary Consul*, the Central Intelligence Agency (CIA) of the United States is on hand to watch as dissidents are tortured. One of the story's kidnappers, who squealed only after three of his fingers had been cut off, tells of his experience: "The counterinsurgency section of the CIA was pleased with me. Two of their agents were there, and they gave me three packets of Lucky Strike. A packet for each man I had betrayed" (Greene 1973, 127).

In *Travels with My Aunt*, on a ship taking him to Asunción, the main character, Henry Pulling, meets an agent who is "kind of . . . not exactly" (Greene 1969, 213) in the CIA, who calls himself James O'Toole. "Do you find things easy in Paraguay? I've read in the papers you Americans have a lot of trouble in South America," Pulling asks. "Not in Paraguay," O'Toole responds. "'We and the General are like that.' He raised his thumb and forefinger and then transferred them to his refilled glass" (Greene 1969, 176). From Greene's perspective, wherever you are in Paraguay, there is a pervasive sense of danger, and the police and other quasi-authorities function with impunity. On the other hand, the Catholic critic of US foreign policy seemed to enjoy his encounters there:

> It is a country of exiles. Graham Greene loved it. He lived and wrote at the Hotel Gran del Paraguay in Asuncion, a fading colonial relic which manages the undemanding achievement of having the best restaurant in Paraguay. (Higham 2006)

In *Paradise Mislaid: In Search of the Australian Tribe of Paraguay*, her book about the descendants of the settlers of the 1890s, Anne Whitehead ([1997] 2018) refers often to Greene, a decision that causes skeptical reviewer Naomi Parry (1997) to complain, "Most disconcerting is Whitehead's habit of drawing analogies between herself and writers such as Graham Greene—that is a pedestal too tall." However, Whitehead merely shows how in *The Honorary Consul* and *Travels with My Aunt*, Greene correctly and interestingly portrays aspects of the Paraguay she encounters on her travels there. In the light of decades of subsequent history, the Australians' decision to pick Paraguay for their new home seems unfortunate since those emigrants who remained, and in particular their sons and daughters who were born there, including Rose Summerfield's son, León Cadogan, were often forced under the domination of Stroessner to function within an oppressive atmosphere characterized by censorship and some of the most egregious human rights abuse. Nonetheless, despite the presence of an official cultural bias against radical and indigenous literary forms that prevented their promotion, and could lead to imprisonment, León enjoyed some official tolerance for a time, which allowed him to translate and publish the *Ayvu Rapyta*, an important document of Guaraní culture and other works (Harvey 2010, 305; Saguier 1979, 27–31).

In the case of the New Australia settlement, and to a lesser extent, that of Cosme, there were always Australians who decided they had made a mistake, and in many instances they were unable to afford to travel back home, which found them seeking financial assistance to enable them to book passage on a ship. Reports such as the following did little to suggest that the new society was in any way a successful enterprise, even though leaders of the New Australia movement constantly tried to deny that more than just a few of their members were unhappy:

> Commissioner Coombes, of the Salvation Army, has received a cable from the Army authorities in Buenos Ayres that there are twenty destitute families who went to New Australia there, who are pleading for assistance to carry them back to the colonies. The Army is providing shelter for a number of the unfortunates, and Commissioner Coombes asks that the Premier of New South Wales be informed of their wishes, and desires to know whether the Government or public will raise funds to pay their passages back. ("Telegrams" 1894)

In fact, the previous premier, Sir George Dibbs, who had now been succeeded by George Reed, had some months before authorized the expenditure of public funds for this purpose ("New Australia" 1894d).

William Stewart, the British Consul in Paraguay reported in April 1894 that some of 110 colonists who had abandoned the "New Australia" colony had unsuccessfully asked him to pay for their passage to Buenos Aires; only six of them could afford to do this by themselves ("New Australia" 1894). Many others sought repatriation and struggled to find a way to finance it. In 1897, six families received assistance from the Queensland government to return to their colony, arriving on the *Duke of Argyll*, some disembarking as the ship arrived in each port, specifically Townsville, Rockhampton, Maryborough, and finally Brisbane. This was apparently a long journey since the *Duke of Argyll* had left London around two months earlier, on June 6, 1897, and it must have taken some additional months for the returnees to travel from Paraguay to London ("Duke of Argyll" N.d.; "Pilgrims from Paraguay: More Disgusted New Australians" 1897).

Similarly disheartened a few years later, in 1902, Rose wrote a letter from her new home in Las Ovejas to the editor of the Sydney area *Worker*, in which she referred to presently drought-stricken Paraguay as "a land of delays and disappointments" where she and her family were waiting for an opportunity to improve their situation, for example, she noted, by returning to Australia. Her husband had been involved in building a school in Las Ovejas, and children there were being taught Spanish and English ("The Cadogans in Exile" 1902). The next year, a report appeared in the same weekly which highlighted comments that Rose had made in a more recent letter. This time, she seemed much more optimistic, apparently commenting that settlers who had returned to Queensland now wanted to go back to Paraguay where "[l]iving is so easily got and the life is so free" ("News from Paraguay" 1903). Her family now possessed a piano, and the settlers worried that their children, in learning the local Guaraní language, would be exposed explicitly to characteristics of adult behavior. The persistence of Guaraní in the area, despite the presence of Spanish, Portuguese, and English, appears to be a unique phenomenon. Perez (2016, 161) writes that "the Anglo-Paraguayan settlement project may be the only case in the colonial history of English in which a speech community shifted from its English heritage language to a local indigenous one."

On the other hand, in her poem, "Australia," Rose reveals more disappointment with Paraguay, sixteen years after she embarked upon a new life adventure, at what had become her sadness at being exiled so far from her native land:

> Not all the thousand fond delights
> My love from thee could e'er beguile, Australia,
> I am longing for my own land,
> My dear land, my home land;
> I'm sighing for its peaceful shore. (Summerfield 1915)

From the start, a certain amount of skepticism had been evinced about the settlement project and of the motives of its champions. Isaacs notes:

> The venture was the first significant emigration from Australia. It attracted derision from many. The *Bulletin* magazine, then at its height of nationalistic influence, for instance, constantly ridiculed the venture. Many in the working class saw the project as a cop-out from fighting for better conditions in Australia. Even the Brisbane *Worker*, Lane's former newspaper, opposed the project. (Isaacs 2015)

An article in the April 8, 1890, issue of a journal of economics and shipping called the *Review of the River Plate*, which a couple of months later was picked up by the Adelaide *Advertiser*, mocked even what it termed "the somewhat grandiloquent title of the 'New Australia Co-operative Settlement Association,' which of itself," the writer continued, "should deter would-be associates from investing their hard-earned savings without very careful investigation" ("A Futile Search for Utopia" 1893). When the association's agent, Gilbert Casey (who would become the chief of police at New Australia), addressed a meeting at the Theatre Royal in Brisbane in 1893, he tried to tackle the claim of other Australians that going to Paraguay (and thus leaving Australia) was "cowardice," though he argued that it would have been better to assemble New Australia in Australia itself. In Paraguay, unlike Queensland, he continued, it would be possible to make laws that would promote justice, and they had already secured land for free (Stubbs 2012; Sullivan 1979; "The 'New Australia' Settlement in Paraguay" 1893).

Positive reports constantly refuted those of critics dissatisfied with the Paraguay experience. On March 22, 1895, a resident of the Cosme settlement named Harry wrote to his Uncle John. In his letter, he told of the "happy-go-lucky Spaniards," who might in the light of their casual attitude be the cause of previous mail he had sent to relatives back home being undelivered or otherwise ending up in the wrong hands. On the other hand, he noted, "I do not think there are many countries in the world with greater possibilities than Paraguay for extended agricultural settlement." Optimistically, Harry pointed out that the commune was now producing almost all its own food, with only minimal exceptions such as salt and yerba maté, the herbal beverage prized by locals now enjoyed by the settlers, having to be purchased, a satisfactory situation given that the settlers were short of currency ("Paraguay: The Cosme Settlement" 1895). In 1897, "a Young New Australian" reported positively on the Paraguay experience, describing a country where water, oranges, and other fruits were plentiful and easily accessed. Interaction with the locals was pleasant and offered opportunities for cultural experimentation. For example:

> They drink "mate" [maté] nearly all day. Now this "mate" or "yerba" as it is called before it is made, can only be grown in one or two spots in Paraguay, and

> is a green powder with the sticks of the plant in it, and in taste it is very bitter, but you can acquire a liking for it, and some of the New Australians would have it in preference to tea. The Paraguayans do not take it as we do. They have a small cup made from the "calabash," which grows there, and half fill it with "yerba," then pour boiling water into it and suck it through a tube. Taken in this way it is very strong but still does not affect the nerves. ("Some Good Points of Paraguay and New Australia" 1897)

Mary Cameron (1865–1962), one of the settlers, arrived in Paraguay in January 1896, joining Lane at Cosme, where she served as a teacher and edited the *Cosme Monthly* newsletter, marrying William Gilmore with whom she had a son. She returned to Australia, where she would be famous as a poet, become Dame Mary Gilmore, and have her portrait featured on the $10 note ("Colonia Nueva Australia and Colonia Cosme in Paraguay" 2012; Hannan 1966, 180–183; Symes 2004). In 1916, she complained that:

> [T]he remaining settlers in Cosme colony—about twelve families—would be very pleased if they could return to Australia. But they would need assistance to make the passage. All their boys of military age have gone to the front, and they are beginning to find that Paraguay is a very good place to get out of, and Australia, with all its faults, is a very good place to return to. ("New Paraguay" 1916)

However, Gilmore at different times evinced contradictory opinions about the success or failure of the Cosme experience, while praising William Lane, who from others has received rather more criticism than praise. Like Lane, she became substantially more conservative in her later years after leaving Cosme (Harvey 2010, 301–302). Surprisingly, despite that curve in her views, she defended the ideals that had governed life at Cosme but failed at New Australia:

> No men who lived in Cosme ever wrote against Communism or against William Lane. The published complaints and misrepresentations all came from those who, ceasing to be Communists, had remained at Las Ovejas, the original settlement. ("Mary Gilmore Tells of Cosme" 1952)

When Lane and his *Royal Tar* party arrived at the area to be used for the commune in 1893, he sent a cable to the New Australia Co-Operative Settlement Association back home that "All arrived in good health. Taken possession of land. Are delighted with the country, and perfectly satisfied with the site granted." However, the truth was that everything was already not at all well, and actually a female infant aged nine months had died on the ship. Increasingly, settlers sent letters to relatives back home in Australia, denouncing Lane as a dictator, and recounting the many disputes between their neighbors ("New Australia" 1893; Painter N.d.; "The New Australia Settlement" 1893; "The New Australia Settlement: Safe Arrival at Paraguay" 1893). Over the next quarter of a century, the extent of the project's profound failure would be discussed and analyzed by many ordinary members of the public. In a letter to the *Auckland Star*, a person describing himself only as a "British Workman," wrote:

> Before they got half-way to their destination they started to quarrel among themselves, and it was stated that stand-up fights took place aboard the Royal Tar. At any rate, within two years, this model party of Socialists, or what was left of them, implored the Government to send a boat and bring them back to Australia. An ounce of practice is worth a ton of theoretical talk. Paraguay is a splendid country in every respect, so I am given to understand; and men who are not afraid of work, and who possess a little common sense, can succeed there. ("British Workman" 1911)

William Lane was born in Bristol, England, on September 6, 1861, with most researchers saying that he attended Bristol Grammar School, although there is some inconsistency as to where he was educated, including a myth that he was so intelligent he was admitted to Oxford University at the age of 14 (Souter [1968] 2012, 26), with Livermore (1950, 291) stating that he attended "Colston Grammar School." Livermore could be referencing the curiously named Colston Hospital, a boys' boarding school founded by philanthropist slave trader Edward Colston in Bristol in 1710, which is now known as Colston's School. In 2020, Colston's statue was hurled into the city's harbor as part of an anti-racist protest (Elmi 2020). When in 1924, William's brother, John "Jack" Lane, gave a lecture about the settlements to an audience of teachers in the Brisbane area, he said that his brother had been educated at "the Bristol Grammar School," a phraseology that does not help resolve the issue, since there were several institutions of the type in Bristol at the time ("The New Australia: Paraguay and Cosme" 1924). Despite the fact that much more material and research interest has accrued to Lane and his brothers, the settlements in Paraguay, and their origins and aftermaths than is the case with respect to the life and thought of Rose Summerfield, contradictory factual details about these subjects are often evident.

William Lane used pseudonyms, such as "John Miller," the apparent author's name of his book "*The Workingman's Paradise: An Australian Labour Novel*" (Lane [1892] 2005), which he wrote while involved as a union organizer with the Australian Labor Federation (ALF) in the Shearers' Strike of 1891 in Queensland. Another name, "Lucinda Sharpe," which appeared on various newspaper columns in the colony, has been attributed to

William, but other researchers believe that those contributions were actually scribed by his wife, Anne (Bowden and Bowden 2004, 84; Kellett 1997, 12; Thompson 2013). Fellow journalist, Edinburgh, Scotland-born Anne "Annie" McQuire met and married Lane when she was working for a newspaper in either Chicago, Illinois (Thompson 2013) or else Detroit, Michigan (Souter [1968] 2012, 26) (sources differ) in the early 1880s; Kellett (1997, 1) avoids committing to a particular city, saying just that they had "met and married in the United States." In 1885, Annie, who was generally, in the manner of the times, referred to only as "Mrs. Lane," traveled with him to Brisbane, and in 1893 she accompanied him to the New Australia settlement in Paraguay. The marriage lasted until her husband died in 1917 in Auckland, New Zealand, their new home (Reeve 1926; Thompson 2013).

William Lane seems not to have consistently held any particular political ideological allegiance, which is interesting given the tendency of some critics of the Paraguay settlements and their underlying dogmas to attribute their apparent failure to the impracticality of communism, a belief system to which at times he expressed his commitment and described as a form of religious faith ("Brooklyn Pastor on 'Better America'" 1922; "Ex-Socialist" 1913; "How Does It Work?" 1920; "Socialistic Colonies" 1894). While not exactly condemning Lane's achievement outright, the Washington, DC, *Evening Times* reflected as follows:

> All intending Cosme settlers must absolutely accept communistic principles and be total abstainers. They must too, deposit a sum of money sufficient to pay their return ticket. In the colony all property is common and money is not used. William Lane, an Australian, was the founder of Cosme, which is one of the very few communist settlements which have not proved absolute failures. ("Relieved from the Tax Man" 1900)

Other commentators portray Lane, notwithstanding his personal flaws, as unswerving, a man "whose love of power, inability to face criticism and self-righteous conviction of his own destiny made him incapable of governing his little society in Paraguay" (Livermore 1950, 313):

> There can be no question that Lane really believed what he said. He himself put all his savings into the association. Most of those who knew him regarded him as the soul of honor. (Livermore 1950, 297)

However, his brother Ernie recalled a time when William had expressed strongly conservative, religious, patriotic beliefs:

> When he had left England for America some years before he had given me as a parting gift a Church of England prayer book in the fly leaf of which he had

written "Fear God and Honour the King." That was the very foundation of our moral and spiritual life. I reminded him of this. He had forgotten, and I said sadly, "Don't you believe that now?" He laughed and replied "No!" And you won't some day when you know better." (Lane [1939] 1993, 26–27; see also Souter [1968] 2012, 26, 28)

For Campbell, who cites Ernie's opinion, Will Lane's true commitments eventually emerged from beneath a shadow of conservatism inculcated by his influential father:

> Lane came from a petty bourgeois family which emerged from a peasant environment in Ireland. His father was an active Tory and in his young days Lane was strongly influenced by his views. Some years spent in America however, helped to change his ideas and when he arrived in Australia in the middle 'eighties he was a confirmed socialist. (Campbell 1945)

Ironically, in the final period of his life, as an editor in New Zealand, he appears to have returned to something like these same reactionary principles. The exceptions, of course, would be his commitments to keeping the Paraguayan settlements (1) whites only and (2) teetotal—the former belief consistent with that of others in the Australian labor movement, and the latter influenced by his reaction to his father's heavy drinking (Whitehead [2003] 2018, 17). McKernan (2012) writes, "Son of an alcoholic, he could not abide drinkers." These views may never have changed while he otherwise veered in contradictory directions as his life and the countries in which he was presently living changed.

For William Lane, Cosme was governed by a principle that he referred to as "communism," a view that was shared by a resident who wrote to the Perth newspaper, the *West Australian*. Concerned that professional journalists in Australia and the United Kingdom had failed to pay sufficient attention to the nature of the colony, the writer described the meaning of the word in some detail, as follows:

> For the sake of those not conversant with our history, it will be needful to state that Cosme is a co-operative settlement of English-speaking people located in Paraguay. It was founded rather more than five years ago by a party of Australians, and has since been joined by various people from Britain. The aim of Cosme is to restore in fuller measure than of old the free house life which for generations have been weakening amongst the English; to rebuild on foundations of broadest fellowship, the village commune which bred the freedom-loving hardihood of our Saxon forefathers; to gather once more into family kinship and unite in the bonds of brotherhood the hearthless and the

> landless of our race; and to win again the lost birthright of the Englishman—a place among his own people. ("Cosme Colony" 1900)

This messianic prioritization of returning to a golden Saxon age under which the loss of individual freedom masquerades as a higher form of liberty is perhaps an accurate description of Lane's beliefs, but it does not sound like communism; in fact, it sounds much more like fascism.

Having departed the Cosme settlement in June 1899, around the time that Rose Summerfield and her family would arrive, Lane headed to New Zealand. In Auckland, where he briefly for the first time edited the conservative newspaper the *New Zealand Herald*, he soon became viewed again as a major journalist. Following a short return to Australia in 1900 to serve as the editor of the Sydney area *Worker*, he returned to New Zealand and became an editorial writer for the *Herald*. As Isaacs (2015) notes, "[I]t is believed he left [the *Worker*] because his views were no longer compatible with those of the Labour movement." Back in New Zealand, his columns took on an extremely anti-union, jingoistic, or anti-German tone, advocating compulsory military service. This became particularly the case after his son, Cpl. Donald Lane, was killed in 1915 during the Gallipoli landing in the First World War. William Lane died on August 26, 1917, having been editor of the *Herald* again since 1913 (Isaacs 2015; "Personal" 1917; Schwarz 2016; Souter [1968] 2012, 254–255, 278–283; "The Late Mr. William Lane" 1917; Thompson 2013; Untitled 1920.) Souter comments on the phenomenal change in Lane's views:

> From 1900 until his death in 1917, Lane contributed to the *Herald* not only as leader-writer, but from 1913 onwards as editor, but also under the penname of "Tohunga," the Maori word for prophet. His editorials gave short shrift to industrial lawlessness. (Souter [1968] 2012, 279–280)

In fact, as far as labor unions were concerned, he condemned them for their "presumption that a 'class war' constantly exists" (280), an idea that "is utterly foreign to British peoples and is alien to the cool thought and considered judgment of British workers" (280). For Bruce Scates, Lane had essentially now abandoned his prior beliefs:

> By 1913 the one time Utopian was the editor of a conservative Auckland daily. By then there was little socialism left in William Lane: even the rhetoric of mateship was appropriated by the militarist fervour of the day. With the outbreak of war, Lane urged diggers onto the beaches of Gallipoli with the same zeal he had once beckoned bushmen to the jungles of Paraguay. (Scates 1990, 55)

Curiously, the Christchurch, N.Z. *Star* editorialized about this transformation following Lane's death as follows:

> Experience and the passing of years mellowed William Lane's views, and although the position of editor of New Zealand's leading Conservative journal seemed a curious contradiction to his ardent ultra-socialistic career in Australia and South America, his public was the gainer by the wide knowledge of men and the wisdom begotten of trials and failures that tempered his writings. ("Current Topics: The Pioneer of 'New Australia'" 1917)

While Lane's skills may or may not have been improved by the variety of his life experience, the notion of a person having "mellowed" into jingoistic ranting is a somewhat unusual point of view. Nonetheless, the editor's professional skills during his final epoch were widely acknowledged. When Hector Bolitho, a New Zealand journalist who had been working in London for 14 years and achieved some success, returned to Auckland and met with local newspaper reporters, he credited the late William Lane with helping him develop his own writing expertise ("Mr. Hector Bolitho: Journalists' Welcome" 1934).

For Kellett, on the other hand, who realizes his article is challenging the orthodox portrayal, Lane's philosophy was actually coherent as he adhered to its guideposts throughout his life. Kellett argues that, far from going to Paraguay to escape the social and economic disadvantages encountered by most Australians at the time, Lane was advancing his millenarian perspective, to which he refers as "sentimental socialism" (Kellett 1997, 7, 8, 9):

> And just as Adam and Eve's expulsion from Eden resulted from their having overstepped the bounds which were established through their covenant with God, so too the demise of William Lane and his Utopian socialism can be seen as the product of his overstepping the bounds of "mateship"—neither in the Garden of Eden nor in the Paraguayan jungle was there room for a New Christ. In the end, William Lane could not be a "mate" except, perhaps, to his wife. (Kellett 1997, 16)

Notwithstanding his fascinating and well-argued portrayal of Lane, Kellett says nothing about the latter's initial traditionalist Christian fervor or his ultimate militaristic ultraconservatism. McKernan, on the other hand, prefers to construct a biography of failure:

> Lane called his settlement New Australia and he left it somewhat more quickly than he had left the original. Really, he was booted out. So, with those who still believed in him he started again at a place he called Cosme. When that staggered into failure, too, Lane lost heart in the idea of paradise, or Utopia as

> he had called it, and set off for New Zealand where he reinvented himself as a conservative. It is a sad and essentially wasted life but the tragedy was more the disruption and difficulties he caused his followers. (McKernan 2012)

In May 1893, for the purpose of ferrying its members to Paraguay, the "New Australia" Committee purchased a sailing ship of a type commonly at the time referred to as a "barque" for £1650; the vessel was the *Royal Tar*, and since its construction around 1880, it had already amassed a notable history, including being denied access to San Francisco when its crew succumbed to malaria, and US authorities argued, unsuccessfully, that the ship should be sunk. When the *Royal Tar* left Sydney on July 16, 1893, watched as it left by Mary Cameron and other supporters, it carried the first batch of "New Australia" recruits, a total of 239 persons, disembarking in Montevideo as of September 12. Following transit by the steamer *Rio Parana* and then on bullock carts, they arrived at the settlement on October 4; the numbers given in different reports about the numbers of *Royal Tar* passengers often differ to a small degree ("Australians Colonising Paraguay" 1893; Livermore 1950, 299; "New Australia: Arrival of the Pioneers: A Second Detachment" 1893; "New Australia: Career of the Rayol [*sic*] Tar." 1923; "'New Australia' Expedition: First Contingent Sailed" 1893; "The New Australia Scheme: The Settlement at Paraguay" 1893; Whitehead [2003] 2018, 12).

Later that month, negative appraisals from some of these initial settlers prompted William Lane to decide not to allow any women on the pending next trip back to Paraguay by the *Royal Tar*, and he sent a cable to W. W. Head in Sydney that said, "Delay all women for six months; send bushmen with all possible despatch" and the "cargo" was changed to 200 single men. On December 28, 1893, the ship was reported to have left, following a stop at Adelaide, with approximately that number of men bound for the Paraguay settlement, plus about 24 women and children. Knowing little about the conflict that had developed on the ship's previous voyage, many of the emigrants this time were suddenly alarmed when, warned that they would be expelled from the association if they did not take a bath, they glimpsed the autocratic nature of some of their leaders; consequently, when the barque arrived, a few decided to return straightaway to Australia ("Australian" 1893; Hannan 1966, 129–130; Livermore 1950, 306; "New Australia: Another Batch of Immigrants" 1893; "New Australia: Arrival of the Pioneers: A Second Detachment" 1893; "New Australia: News from Paraguay" 1893). By the beginning of May 1894, the *Royal Tar* was in South Australia, amid plans to go back to Paraguay with a shipload of female settlers, a project to be organized by Annie Lane, who had returned on the ship with that purpose in mind. However, conflict between the existing settlers and their split into two differently oriented communes—the Saints (or Royalists) and the Sinners (or Rebels), the Saints moving to Cosme, to the south, on the Pirapó River—meant that, although the efforts to attract more emigrants continued, and new people arrived as others left, there were no more voyages to Paraguay on the *Royal Tar* ("New Australia" 1894e, 1927; Prior 1907; "Return of the Royal Tar: Arrangements for a Shipment of Women" 1894; Stubbs 2012). Mary Cameron Gilmore described the exodus whereby Lane and the true believers departed:

> The idealist ruled the division; and about sixty persons set out with three weeks' provisions, about thirty head of cattle, and a horse or two, to seek new land. Almost penniless, they camped, night after night, in a strange land, of whose very language most of them were ignorant, but at last, their provisions almost done, they found land they could have for purchase. . . . With that, the new colony, Cosme, started—nine leagues of land, monte, camp, and estero. (Gilmore 1909)

To build some capital, the Cosme settlers sold their jewelry, wedding rings excepted. As they waited for the maize they had quickly planted in the new plot of land to grow, and which, in the absence of electric power, they would have to grind by hand, they lived on beans ("'New Australia' in Paraguay" 1895; "The Cosme Colony: Lecture in Gloucester" 1897; "The New Australia: Paraguay and Cosme" 1924). Their goal was the more rigid moral code that had failed in New Australia, abstinence from alcohol and from cohabitation with Paraguayans, with a lifelong commitment to marriage bonds (Isaacs 2015; "New Australia" 1894d; "The Colony at Cosme: Progress of the English Community in Paraguay" 1901; "The Cosme Colony: Lecture in Gloucester" 1897). Advocates now claimed that Cosme was the Holy Grail, with an ideal system of government, and Lane the perfect leader:

> When the unfortunate split took place, it did not destroy Will Lane's faith in humanity and in the possibility of men finding a more human and natural way of life than is seen anywhere yet. . . . I, for one, have faith in Lane, and believe that he will yet be the means of giving the world a much-needed object lesson in how to live simpler, purer, and consequently happier lives. (W. G. 1895)

However, it might be asked what is denoted by "pure." Is it a traditional family life where women concentrate on household duties, losing their right to vote and work outside the home when they marry, becoming second-class citizens? That situation, actualized at Cosme, was far less emancipating than had been anticipated by William Lane when he wrote that "[a] woman has every bit a right to work and to live as a man has" (Lane, quoted by Scates 1990, 50). Life at Cosme was also, as Mary Cameron discovered, less advanced than the circumstances at the Welsh settlement in Patagonia,

Argentina, named "Y Wladfa" ("The Colony") where everyone over the age of 18 could vote, regardless of marital status (Whitehead [2003] 2018, 41). Yet Jack Lane, who had been a teacher at Cosme and later took over its leadership, claimed that "[g]overnment of the colony was absolutely democratic" ("The New Australia: Paraguay and Cosme" 1924). The rationalization for this was apparently that, as Hannan (1966, 166) notes, "the family was taken as the basic unit of the colony." As a place where even the decision whether or not to drink alcohol was no longer a matter of individual choice, Cosme's perfect way of life often seems oppressive.

Information about Colonia Cosme was circulated by *Cosme Monthly*, a handwritten four-page publication, copies of which were mailed from time to time to friends and relatives back in Australia, and details found in the journal were then sometimes reported to local newspapers. *Cosme Monthly* provided informative statistics about the residents and some evidence about how the enterprise was being organized. Reportedly, in 1896, Cosme had 49 men, 19 women, and 27 children. By February 1901, according to *Cosme Monthly*, it had a smaller population of men: 28 men, 18 women, and 37 children. The journal reported frustration with persons who had joined the colony "solely for the material benefits" ("Cosme" 1901a). By July 7 of the same year, the adult population had dwindled again, to 25 men and 16 women, but there were 46 children. In the fall, Jack Lane was back in Australia, seeking recruits and selling photographs of the settlement, while praising the successful regime of "communism" where the hunger experienced in Australia no longer occurred, but where children growing up in the settlement had no familiarity with the retail environment, and the school facilities, although they succeeded in teaching the English language, were generally inadequate. By 1902, *Cosme Monthly* was reporting that a cooperative bakery had been set up, under the management of Alec Lewis. As more settlers left, the newsletter was reduced to a quarterly publication, while colony watchers speculated that the enterprise would soon fail ("Colonia Cosme Items" 1902; "Colonia Cosme: News From Paraguay" 1896; "Cosme" 1901a, 1901b, 1904). Nonetheless, the colony at Cosme survived as a collectivist enterprise until 1909, when the property was changed into individual holdings and paperwork certifying the change was signed; a similar transformation occurred at New Australia. During the First World War, many of the younger male residents of the transformed Colonia Cosme enlisted in the U.K. or Australian military, perhaps a sign of their continuing emotional ties to the place from whence their parents came ("Colonia Nueva Australia and Colonia Cosme in Paraguay" 2012; "Cosme" 1901b; "New Australia's Part" 1916; Symes 2004). Elizabeth Christensen (2018), an American descendant of Cosme residents with roots in Australia, notes that "[i]n the end only eight families remained in Cosme, including my own."

Disputes between settlers had begun during the first voyage of the *Royal Tar*. Clara Jones, an unmarried nurse unaccompanied by her parents, made the mistake of sitting out on the deck after 8 p.m., an apparent offense against morality that prompted its prohibition, an act that in turn was overruled by a meeting of settlers who instead regarded the matter as one of individual liberty, which caused William Lane, anxious to preserve every scrap of his power, to threaten to resign. It quickly became apparent that consumption of alcohol, if discovered, would not be tolerated. In Montevideo, when the *Royal Tar* arrived concluding its first trip, settlers were forced to throw away a container of molasses because it contained a minute quantity of alcohol (Hannan 1966, 100–101; Martyn 1926; Reeve 1926). Later, when three of the residents (Tom Westwood, Louis Simon, and Fred White) traveled to a neighboring village and returned bearing evidence that they had been drinking, Lane ordered them expelled and refused to reconsider his decision. He went to Asunción, fetching government officials and six armed police officers, who forced the men in question to leave. Such heavy-handedness prompted the split between the residents, with Lane and his allies leaving, and Frederick Kidd being elected the new leader of New Australia ("Letters from Paraguay" 1894; Martyn 1926; "New Australia" 1894a, 1894b, 1894c; "New Australia: Settlement News" 1894; Reeve 1926; "The New Australia" 1894; "The Paraguay Temperance Settlement" 1893).

An editorial that appeared in the South Australia newspaper, the *Kadina and Wallaroo Times*, emphasized the irony of millenarian philosophies tending to require enforcement by dictators, a phenomenon of which New Australia was but the latest example:

> The New Australian Paraguayan millenium, which was to be a working model for all future milleniums, has only lasted for thirteen weeks. The government, which was to be based on principles of pure reason and general consent, has already come short in the latter requisite. No doubt the edicts of Lane, the dictator, are the outcome of pure reason, but it has been found necessary to produce a loaded revolver in order to secure the general consent. By-and-by other people will emphasise their dissent by the use of revolvers, and then the settlement will not be ruled by an apostle of lofty principle and pure reason like Lane, but by the best shot. The settlers are reduced, according to the statement of the man who has been sent out to explain why it has gone wrong, to a diet of bread and meat. How must the shearers amongst them look back with regret to the day when they were supplied by the hated capitalistic squatter with five meals a day, in addition to unlimited tea and "brownie" [a currant bread]. ("Paraguay Settlement" 1894)

In addition to Lane's autocratic leadership and his extremist's dislike of alcohol use, New Australia's family-oriented structure and "whites only" philosophy made dalliances and relationships with the locals another ground for expulsion. Among the Paraguayans, there was a surfeit of women, and among the settlers, there were too many single men. The colonists had tried to recruit women in England in order to lessen this gender imbalance, but when it did not transpire, some of the men left ("Cosme Colony" 1900). Once "a serpent in the shape of the local Eve . . . entered into the Socialist paradise" ("Local & General" 1894), the negative effects caused outrage among the Australian women. One of the settlers who left New Australia, A. Brittlebank, complained also that Lane had failed to provide a settlement balance sheet, while those who chose to leave were subjected to a humiliating search of their personal effects. Meanwhile, the indigenous Paraguayans were being moved away from the area of the original settlement to make room for those who would arrive on the second trip of the *Royal Tar*, ethnic cleansing which would also have the effect of separating the locals from the orchards of oranges surrounding their homes, from which they had historically derived nourishment and income ("New Australia" 1894e).

Originally, unable to obtain a suitable location in New South Wales or another of the Australasian colonies, the plan had been for the New Australia Co-Operative Settlement Association to purchase land in Argentina and, in 1891, its leaders sent Alf Walker, who had been involved with William Lane on the *Boomerang*, to negotiate with that country's government. However, the appeal of much more favorable terms available in Paraguay, where that nation's government, anxious to replace the citizens killed in its crushing defeat in the 1864–1870 Triple Alliance War by Brazil, Argentina, and Uruguay, at the end of which only 14,000 Paraguayan men were left alive, offered the would-be emigrants 450,000 acres free of charge in addition to covering some of the surveying and other costs. The association hoped to have 10,000 residents by the end of the century. Under the original terms, settlers were asked to contribute £60 to New Australia's funds ("A Futile Search for Utopia" 1893; González de Bosio 2010, 85–86; Hannan 1966, 63, 76; Mawson 2011, 95; "New Australia" 1893; Schwarz 2016; Souter [1968] 2012, 55).

Rose died on Good Friday, 1922. Reports in Australian newspapers at the time recorded her departure, but tended to lessen her importance:

> In the early days of the Labor Movement, before the advent of the Labor Party, when a strenuous propaganda was carried on on Sunday evenings at Leigh House, Mrs. Summerfield was a well-known attendant and lecturer. She also did some organising among the women workers, and was a frequent contributor to the "Worker." ("Death of a Labor Pioneer" 1922)

Even a story that listed a number of details of her life and recalled her "brilliant addresses at the Sunday night meetings held at Leigh House, Sydney, a generation ago" ("Death of Rose Summerfield" 1922), summed up her significance only as follows:

> Better known as Rose Summerfield, Mrs Cadogan was prominent in Australian Labor circles in the nineties of last century as Socialist lecturer and writer and Labor organizer. ("Death of Rose Summerfield" 1922)

At that time, her surviving husband, Jack Cadogan, wanted to go back to Australia, but could not afford to do so, although three of their sons, Eric, Bronte, and half-brother Harry Summerfield, had already moved to the Northern Territory where, perhaps given their Paraguayan experiences, they were attracted to the Outback environment. Four years later, a report in the *Windsor and Richmond Gazette* confirmed that the remaining Cadogans' predicament had not changed:

> Mr. Jack Cadogan and his son Leon, (born at New Australia, 1899) who nowadays resides at Villa Rica, Paraguay, are stressing the urge for the Federal Ministry to send over a ship and bring those people back who left Australia; and there are others resident at New Australia, just as anxious to return, but their resources will not permit. (Reeve 1926)

Around the same time, León Cadogan wrote to a correspondent as follows: "Father and I would dearly like to get back to Australia, but it is out of the question at present. We have very few ties with the Motherland—Australia" (Molesworth 1926). In response to this entreaty, Voltaire "Vol" Molesworth editorialized as follows:

> And the echo of William Lane's madness comes from the dirty, lazy environs of Villa Rica with Leon Cadogan's plea for repatriation to his Motherland. (Molesworth 1926)

The next year, a Cosme resident named William Wood, who was one of the original New Australia settlers, lamented Jack's gradual physical decline (Reeve 1926):

> Poor old Jack Cadogan, he is now well into the sere and yellow. I was told a few days ago that Jack is now almost blind and in very bad health. Vastly different to when I met him in 1894 at Marathon Station near Hughenden, Queensland, where he was cooking for the station hands at that year's shearing. I remember he gave myself and George Whealan a good feed there, and plenty for the track. Jack was hit very hard when Mrs. Cadogan died. ("New Australia" 1927)

On November 22, 1929, Eric Cadogan was killed following a fight with another man, Harry Crosbie, at Adelaide River, NT. Crosbie, whose "half caste" status rendered him, along with others of indigenous ancestry, legally unable to drink alcohol, was often in court on minor charges, particularly following incidents involving his drunkenness. In the case that resulted from his encounter with Eric Cadogan, who was taken to the Darwin Hospital but did not die until December 3, Crosbie was initially charged with assault causing actual bodily harm, and later with murder. At his trial, conducted after Eric had died, a witness called Alfred Victor Stretton testified that he "formed the opinion from the way he [Crosbie] spoke and the way he was walking that he was under the influence of liquor" ("Coroner's Inquiry" 1929). A dispute, he continued, had ensued between Eric and Crosbie over some beef that the latter had left in a paddock and which Cadogan wanted him to immediately deliver elsewhere, but Crosbie refused to do that. Stretton had arrived to discover Eric with a three-inch-long knife wound in his neck, causing his collar bone to protrude, an attack which caused some paralysis. The doctors considered amputating Eric's right arm, but they were obliged to wait until he was well enough to tolerate an operation. Although Eric had been able to give a statement to Court officials, repeated loss of blood caused him to expire more than a week after he had been admitted to the hospital. Even though there were several witnesses, including the prior testimony of the victim, a farmer called John Felstead, who arrived shortly after the incident, could reveal only that Eric had told him that "I made a hit at Crosbie, bumped something and broke my collarbone." Eventually, Crosbie was acquitted. ("A Correction" 1930; "Breakfast Table Quarrel: Leads to Police Court" 1938; "Coroner's Inquiry" 1929; "Darwin Police Court" 1931; "To the Editor" 1929).

Harry Summerfield, who, while living in Paraguay had adopted the name "Enrique," had also returned to Australia, and was bitten by an alligator or crocodile (accounts differ) at Adelaide River in 1920, resulting in substantial damage to both arms and his right leg, which required his hospitalization in Sydney. The creature had started the attack by grabbing his right knee and attempting to pull him into a lagoon, prompting a prolonged fight which Harry eventually survived by repeatedly wounding the crocodile in the eye as it bit him in various places and broke his wrist. Bronte Cadogan died in Turramurra, NSW, in the Sydney area, aged 45 on July 3, 1949 (Souter [1968] 2012, 289, gives the year as 1947), the victim of injuries received during his Second World War service with the Second Australian Imperial Force (AIF) in its New Guinea campaign. Like Eric, Bronte, and Harry, Rose's brother, Joseph "Joe" Stone relocated to the Northern Territory, where he administered Harry's farm as a partner after the latter was unable to work following the encounter with the reptile; Joe was 68 when he died in 1928 (A Narrow Escape: Mauled by a Crocodile" 1922; "Bronte Cadogan" 1949; Cadogan 1935; "Cadogan, Bronte" N.d.; "Death and Burial of Eric Wayne Cadogan" 1929; "Death of a Labor Pioneer" 1922; "Death of Mr. Joe Stone" 1928; "Eric

Cadogan: Died of Wounds in Savage Fight" 1930; "Fight with Alligator: Death Struggle at Adelaide River" 1922; Souter [1968] 2012, 289; "Stone, Joseph" 1928; Whitehead [1997] 2018, 816, 826).

In 1935, León Cadogan sent a letter from Asunción to the Darwin, NT newspaper, the *Northern Standard*, updating some of the details of his family's fortunes and misfortunes. He reported that another brother, Hugh Cadogan, had died of an illness contracted while he was captured by an opposing faction during the Paraguayan Civil War of 1922–1923, the Chirifistas, the supporters of presidential would-be candidate Adolfo Chirife; conflict had erupted after the forthcoming elections were canceled by the incumbent, Eusebio Ayala. Hugh was buried in the same Las Ovejas graveyard in Nueva Londres as his mother (Souter [1968] 2012, 290, 296, 349; Whitehead [1997] 2018, 376–377, 697). In his letter, León, a reservist, said that he would soon be on his way to the Chaco region, the center of a new conflict between Paraguay and Bolivia. Identifying oil and global capitalism as the motive for the fighting, he wrote, "And here we are slaughtering each other by the thousand, all for the glory of the Standard Oil, with the League of Nations looking on, trying to hide a grin" (Cadogan 1935).

Of Rose's five sons, León appears to have been the most successful, despite the repeated frustration of his desire to leave Paraguay and join his surviving brothers. He could speak and translate between English, Spanish, German, and Mbyá-Guaraní, and other dialects spoken by the local Guaraní people, and he composed a Spanish to Mbyá-Guaraní dictionary. His study and knowledge of Guaraní culture and generally sympathetic attitude toward the local people led to them trusting him to write down the *Ayvu Rapyta*, the mythical story that explains their creation in the Atlantic rain forest and that of their language through the actions of four gods, those of fire, sun, mist and shamans, and thunder and water. In his introduction to that work, he conveyed his obvious delight with the results of that project and what they had revealed:

> Mi aporte ha sido el consignar los dictados al papel, y las notas lexicológicas. Y en estas notas reconozco haber abusado de mi condición de profano en ciencias antropológicas al permitirme subrayar algunas, para mi sorprendentes, analogias que he creído hallar entre el contenido de ciertos versos de estos mitos y tradiciones y las grandes religiones de la humanidad. Sabrá tolerármelo el lector, equiparando mis observaciones al alegre grito de sorpresa de quien inesperadamente balla al borde del camino una hermosa flor, o tropieza con una refulgente joya. (Cadogan 1959, 11)

> [My contribution has been to consign the dictations to paper, as well as the lexicological notes. And in these notes I acknowledge having abused my role as layman in the anthropological sciences by taking the liberty of emphasizing some, for me, surprising analogies that I have found between the content of

> certain verses of these myths and traditions and the great religions of humanity. The reader will be able to endure this by treating my remarks as the joyous cry of surprise from someone who unexpectedly finds a beautiful flower on the side of the street, or stumbles upon a glittering jewel.]

León's achievements became celebrated in Paraguay and his visage appeared on an 8,000 guaraní Paraguayan stamp (Ferrari 2020; Harvey 2010, 303–305; Saguier 1979, 29). He died in 1973. Souter writes:

> Don León did better in life than either of his three brothers who returned to Australia. He was described by one eminent Brazilian anthropologist as the foremost authority on Guaraní culture, and although he never became a rich man he was nevertheless able to provide his four children with a good education. (Souter [1968] 2012, 291)

Conclusion

Rose Summerfield, Advocate for Human Dignity

For Mark Hearn (2004, 80), Summerfield's life never blossomed as it might have done:

> The frustrations that Rose experienced also highlighted her relative marginality—she was never accorded a decisive or clear leadership role; only in speeches such as *Master and Man* and the articles and poetry published in the *Hummer/Worker* did she find space to create and project a sustained "voice." Her radicalism often carried the weight of the traditional values it pulled against, and race complicated her radicalism in ways she could not have anticipated. (Hearn 2004, 80)

However, Hearn's assessment seems to be largely inaccurate. Rose's "Master and Man" speech was obviously an important event, and there is much to be learned about her opinions from her extant articles and poems. But to base an ascription of "relative marginality" on some of the information that happens to remain in the twenty-first century is to miss much of her real significance and output. As has been noted in previous chapters of the present work, there is additional published material available about other speeches that she gave, some of which were reported at least partially verbatim, including "The Gospel of Discontent," a performance that is misidentified by Hearn. She did have a "clear leadership role": Summerfield exerted much guidance around Sydney with the Womanhood Suffrage League, chairing many of their meetings, lecturing to their members about a range of different topics, and bringing in visiting speakers to provide additional educational opportunities. She emphasized the concerns of women about the kinds of work they wished to do, the roles they might wish to play within a marriage, and their much neglected need to be treated with respect. She recognized that each family ought to have appropriate housing, realizing that the control of most land and access to it by the wealthy caused many of the poor to languish in slums: to live with dignity, she insisted, they needed space. She was actively involved with other groups and gatherings, with the Australian Socialist League and the Australian Workers' Union, later with teetotalers, and with those coordinating the New Australia movement, promoting her somewhat skeptical version of socialism, her interest in the idea of the single tax, her secular values, and her sympathies for anarchism. She often spoke, read poetry, and sang, and she used her extensive knowledge of serious literature to illuminate her interaction with others, contributing to the intellectual climate of a large city and beyond. She expressed her support for candidates for office, meeting with and criticizing politicians, some of whom were important on a colony-wide level, and attempting to influence policy. She motivated people of casual interest in societal reform, who read her articles and poems, who dropped by meetings and stumbled upon her fine oratory. She worked with union officials, being specifically assigned to solve problems, she found employment for women, and tried to get more women to join the union, and she promoted an eight hour workday. She overcame any meaningful attribution of marginality despite the limits that afflicted women's participation in society in the 1890s through her constant activity and through her thoughtful examination of her own ideological position. By doing all these things, she rendered herself the epitome of a leader, refusing to be tied down to any specific, lessening role. Moreover, she was not a racist in any of the senses generally associated with the terminology that Hearn anachronistically applies, but an advocate for workers and her community and their needs. She was a clear and consistent radical who achieved much improvement in the lives of the people of New South Wales. Until she left for Paraguay in 1899, she was a profound success, and once living there, she tried to help the people she encountered, whether former Australians or disadvantaged locals.

When Hearn (2004, 79) writes that "Paraguay only intensified Rose's alienation," he describes a woman who, while she lived in Sydney, achieved significant prominence due to her unceasing dedication to active participation, argument, and political commitment, someone who was as much involved in local society as anyone else, and thoughtfully so. The ascription of "alienation" to her work and nature seems horribly ill-chosen, and given the attention that Hearn's article has achieved, it is a shame that, while it provides much useful information about its subject, it sadly leaves a false impression of the failure of an important Australian feminist thinker who should actually be much revered.

Bibliography

A Badd Lott. 1898. Letter to the Editor. *Worker* [Wagga, NSW], May 14.
"About the New Woman." 1895. *Daily Telegraph* [Sydney, NSW], February 18.
"A Correction." 1930. *Northern Standard* [Darwin, NT], April 25.
"A Futile Search for Utopia." 1893. *Advertiser* [Adelaide, SA], June 24.
Albeck-Ripka, Livia, and Tariro Mzezewa. 2021. "Locked Up in a Hotel for a Year, Then a Sudden Taste of Freedom." *New York Times*, January 21.
Altgeld, John. [1893] 1915. *Gov. John Altgeld's Pardon of the Anarchists and his Masterly Review of the Haymarket Riot*. Chicago, IL: Lucy Parsons.
"A Narrow Escape: Mauled by a Crocodile." 1922. *Advertiser* [Adelaide, SA], May 3.
Andrade, David A. 1888. "The Chicago Anarchists: A Chapter in History." *Honesty*, February.
Andrade, W. C. 1887. "'Germinal; or, Master and Man': By Emile Zola." *Honesty*, May.
"Australian." 1893. *Evening Post* [Wellington, N.Z.], December 28.
"Australians Colonising Paraguay." 1893. *Colonist* [Nelson, N.Z.], May 23.
"Australian Socialist League." 1892a. *Evening News* [Sydney, NSW], May 19.
"Australian Socialist League." 1892b. *Evening News* [Sydney, NSW], August 25.
"Australian Workers: New Labour Organisation." 1892. *Telegraph* [Brisbane, QLD], November 22.
Avineri, Shlomo. 1968. *The Social and Political Thought of Karl Marx*. Cambridge, U.K.: Cambridge University Press.
Avrich, Paul. 1980. *The Modern School Movement: Anarchism and Education in the United States*. Oakland, CA: AK.
Avrich, Paul. 1984. *The Haymarket Tragedy*. Princeton, NJ: Princeton University Press.
"A Woman Who Heard the Two Lectures." 1892. Letter to the Editor. *Western Herald* [Bourke, NSW], October 15.
"AWU Timeline." 2020. The Australian Workers' Union, National Office, Granville, NSW. https://www.awu.net.au/our-union/history/ (December 14, 2020).
"Back Matter." 2010. *Labour History* 98:286.
Beaumont, Matthew. 2007. "Is It Still Possible to Imagine the Future?" *Guardian*, June 19.

Bellamy, Edward. 1887. *Looking Backward: 2000–1887*. Boston: Houghton Mifflin.

"Ben Tillett." 1898. *Clipper* [Hobart, TAS], February 19.

"Ben Tillett and Melbourne's Mayor." 1898. *Daily News* [Perth, WA], April 23.

"Ben Tillett and the Mayor of Melbourne." 1898. *Worker* [Wagga, NSW], April 9.

Benz, Stephen. 1998. "Graham Greene's Narrative Art: A Case Study in Analyzing Nonfiction Prose." *CEA Critic* 60:6–16.

Benz, Stephen. 2003. "Taking Sides: Graham Greene and Latin America." *Journal of Modern Literature* 26:113–128.

Berkman, Alexander. [1912] 1970. *Prison Memoirs of an Anarchist*. New York: Schocken.

Black, W. F. 1903. "Poverty, always Poverty." *Labour Leader* [Glasgow, U.K.], October 31.

"Black Labor." 1892. *Evening News* [Sydney, NSW], May 30.

Bolton, Geoffrey, and Helen Gregory. 1992. "The 1891 Shearers Strike Leaders: Railroaded?" *Labour History* 62:116–126.

Boncardo, Philip. 2008. "Women, Work and 'Civilised' White Australia: Assessing Responses to Women in Factory and Sweated Labour." B.A. thesis. University of Sydney.

Bongiorno, Frank. 1994. "Class, Populism and Labour Politics in Victoria, 1890–1914." *Labour History* 66:14–32.

Bowden, Bradley. 2009. "No Improvement without Standardisation: The Origins of Queensland's Industrial Relations System, 1857–1916." In *Work and Strife in Paradise: The History of Labour Relations in Queensland 1859 to 2009*, edited by Bradley Bowden, Simon Blackwood, Cath Rafferty, and Cameron Allan. Annandale, NSW: Federation.

Bowden, Bradley. 2011. "The Rise and Decline of Australian Unionism: A History of Industrial Labour from the 1820s to 2010." *Labour History* 100:51–82.

Bowden, Bradley, and Toni Bowden. 2004. "'The Women Do the Machinery': Craft, Gender and Work Transformation in the Brisbane Boot Trade, 1869–95." *Labour History* 86:75–92.

"Breakfast Table Quarrel: Leads to Police Court." 1938. *Northern Standard* [Darwin, NT], November 25.

"Brevities." 1894. *Evening News* [Sydney, NSW], July 2.

"Brevities." 1895. *Evening News* [Sydney, NSW], February 16.

"British Workman." 1911. Letter to the Editor. *Auckland Star* [N.Z.], September 11.

"Bronte Cadogan." 1949. *Windsor and Richmond Gazette* [Windsor, NSW], July 13.

"Brooklyn Pastor on 'Better America.'" 1922. *Wilmington Daily Commercial* [Delaware], February 28.

Bryce, James. 1888. *The American Commonwealth*. New York: Macmillan.

Burgmann, Verity. 1985a. *'In Our Time.' Socialism and the Rise of Labor, 1885–1905*. Sydney, NSW: George Allen & Unwin.

Burgmann, Verity. 1985b. "Who Our Enemies Are: Andrew Markus and the Baloney View of Australian Racism." *Labour History* 47:97–101.

"Cadogan, Bronte." N.d. Virtual War Memorial Australia. https://vwma.org.au/explore/people/580007 (January 10, 2021).

Cadogan, León. 1926. "A Gringo Gaucho in the Yerbales of Paraguay." *Windsor and Richmond Gazette* [Windsor, NSW], March 12.

Cadogan, León. 1935. "A Correspondent's Interesting Letter." *Northern Standard* [Darwin, NT], March 19.

Cadogan, León. 1959. *Ayvu Rapyta*: Textos míticos de los Mbyá Guaraní del Guairá. São Paulo, Brazil: Universidade de São Paulo, Faculdade de Filosofia, Ciências e Letras.

Campbell, E. W. 1945. *History of the Australian Labour Movement: A Marxist Interpretation*. Sydney, NSW: Current. https://www.marxists.org/history/international/comintern/sections/australia/1945/history-labor/index.htm (November 26, 2020).

Carlotta. 1898a. "Branded Children." *Worker* [Wagga, NSW], May 14.

Carlotta. 1898b. "Woman Items." *Worker* [Wagga, NSW], April 30.

"Chinese Labor." 1887. Editorial. *Honesty*, August 28.

Christensen, Elizabeth. 2018. "New Australia, Un Nuevo Mundo." B.A. thesis. California State University, Monterey Bay.

Cirillo, N. R. 1977. "Marxism as Myth in Zola's *Germinal*." *Comparative Literature Studies* 14:244–255.

Claflin, Tennie C. 1898. *Essays on Social Topics*, volume III. Westminster, U.K.: Roxburghe.

Claflin, Tennie C. 1922. *Illegitimacy*. London: Lady Cook [Tennie C. Claflin].

"Colonia Cosme Items." 1902. *North Queensland Register* [Townsville, QLD], March 10.

"Colonia Cosme: News From Paraguay." 1896. *Maryborough Chronicle* [QLD], December 15.

"Colonia Nueva Australia and Colonia Cosme in Paraguay." 2012. http://www.auspostalhistory.com/articles/172.shtml (August 24, 2020).

Conrick, Peter. 1979. *A History of the Australian Labor Party, 1890–1967*. Sydney, NSW: Socialist Workers Party.

Cooper, Rae, and Greg Patmore. 2002. "Trade Union Organising and Labour History." *Labour History* 83:3–18.

"Coroner's Inquiry." 1929. *Northern Standard* [Darwin, NT], December 10.

"Cosme." 1901a. *Arena* [Melbourne, VIC], February 16.

"Cosme." 1901b. *Arena* [Melbourne, VIC], November 28.

"Cosme." 1904. *Westralian Worker* [Perth, WA], January 8.

"Cosme Colony." 1900. *West Australian* [Perth, WA], June 16.

"Current News." 1895. *Newcastle Morning Herald and Miners' Advocate* [NSW], August 19.

"Current Topics: The Pioneer of 'New Australia.'" 1917. Editorial. *Star* [Christchurch, N.Z.], August 27.

"Darwin Police Court." 1931. *Northern Standard* [Darwin, NT], March 3.

Davis, Sue. 2008. *The Political Thought of Elizabeth Cady Stanton: Women's Rights and the American Political Traditions*. New York: New York University Press.

"Death." 1922. *Northern Standard* [Darwin, NT], August 22.

"Death and Burial of Eric Wayne Cadogan." 1929. *Northern Standard* [Darwin, NT], December 6.

"Death of a Labor Pioneer." 1922. *Northern Standard* [Darwin, NT], August 22.

"Death of Mr. Joe Stone." 1928. *Northern Standard* [Darwin, NT], March 27.

"Death of Mrs. J. R. Ashton: A Well-Known Lady Writer" 1900. *Daily Telegraph* [Sydney, NSW], July 16.

"Death of Rose Summerfield." 1922. *Worker* [Brisbane, QLD], August 3.

"Deaths." 1897. "Stone." *Daily Telegraph* [Sydney, NSW], March 18.

DeLamotte, Eugenia C. 2004. *Gates of Freedom: Voltairine de Cleyre and the Revolution of the Mind.* Ann Arbor: University of Michigan Press.

Demack, Alan G. 1991. "The Trials of the Shearers: A Commentary upon the Trial *The Queen v. George Taylor and Others*." Presentation to the meeting of the Capricornia Collection Society. Rockhampton, QLD, May 27.

Doherty, Ben. 2016. "A Short History of Nauru, Australia's Dumping Ground for Refugees." *Guardian*, August 9.

"Duke of Argyll." N.d. Passengers in History: South Australian Maritime Museum. https://passengers.history.sa.gov.au/node/924573 (September 2, 2020).

Dunstan, Alen Katen. 2003. "Landlords, 'Wobblers,' and the Labor Party: Single Taxers in New South Wales; 1883–1898." PhD diss. Macquarie University [Sydney, NSW].

"Editor's Note." 1926. In "A Gringo Gaucho in the Yerbales of Paraguay" by León Cadogan. *Windsor and Richmond Gazette* [Windsor, NSW], March 12.

"Eight Hour Day Monument." 2021. Monument Australia. https://monumentaustralia.org.au/themes/culture/social/display/32235-eig (January 5, 2021).

Elmi, Osob. 2020. "Edward Colston: 'Why the Statue had to Fall.'" BBC News, June 8. https://www.bbc.com/news/uk-england-bristol-52965803 (January 21, 2021).

Epstein, James A. 1985. "The Working Class and the People's Charter." *International Labor and Working-Class History* 28:69–78.

"Eric Cadogan: Died of Wounds in Savage Fight." 1930. *Windsor and Richmond Gazette* [Windsor, NSW], January 3.

"Ex-Socialist." 1913. "Where Socialism Failed." *Evening Post* [Wellington, N.Z.], July 29.

Eyerman, Ron. 1981. "False Consciousness and Ideology in Marxist Theory." *Acta Sociologica* 24:43–56.

Faustine. 1894. "Passing Notes." *Daily Telegraph* [Sydney, NSW], May 19.

Faustine. 1895. "Passing Notes." *Daily Telegraph* [Sydney, NSW], February 23.

Ferrari, Andrea. 2020. "Translating the Ayvu Rapyta: For the Love of a Rainforest and its Word-Souls." *Garland Magazine*, December 1. https://garlandmag.com/article/translating-ayvu-rapyta/ (January 26, 2021).

Fiedler, Klaus. 2016. *The Making of a Maverick Missionary: Joseph Booth in Australasia*. Mzuzu, Malawi: Luviri.

"Fight with Alligator: Death Struggle at Adelaide River." 1922. *Northern Territory Times and Gazette* [Darwin, NT], May 2.

"First a Crawl and Then a Lie." 1892. *Worker* [Wagga, NSW], October 8.

Frances, Raelene. 1999. "Sex Workers or Citizens? Prostitution and the Shaping of 'Settler' Society in Australia." *International Review of Social History* 44:101–122.

"General Gleanings." 1892. *Singleton Argus* [NSW], December 21.

"General Laborers' Union of Australasia." 1893. *Shearers' and General Laborers' Record*, March 15.

George, Henry. [1879] 1912. *Progress and Poverty*. Garden City, NJ: Doubleday, Page. https://www.econlib.org/library/YPDBooks/George/grgPP.html?chapter_num=1#book-reader (November 17, 2020).

Gilmore, Mary. 1909. "Cosme." *Labor Call* [Melbourne, VIC], July 29.

Gollan, Daphne. 1986. "Review of *'In Our Time.' Socialism and the Rise of Labor, 1885–1905* by Verity Burgmann." *Labour History* 51:97–98.

González de Bosio, Beatriz. 2010. *Culture in the Classroom: Teaching Aid Material for Teachers.* Asunción, Paraguay: Secretaria Nacional de Cultura.

"Good Templar Mission." 1896. *Sydney Morning Herald* [NSW], January 30.

"Good Templary." 1896. *Evening News* [Sydney, NSW], March 9.

Gray, Robert. 1986. "The Deconstructing of the English Working Class." *Social History* 11:363–373.

Greene, Graham. 1969. *Travels with My Aunt*. New York: Viking.

Greene, Graham. 1973. *The Honorary Consul*. New York: Simon and Schuster.

"Gundagai." 1892. *Sydney Mail* [NSW], November 19.

"Gundagai, Friday." 1892. *Sydney Morning Herald* [NSW], November 12.

Hannan, John Grant. 1966. "The New Australia Movement." M.A. thesis. University of Queensland.

Harvey, Andrew. 2010. "The Utopian Diaspora: Australians in Paraguay." In *Diasporas: Revisiting and Discovering*, edited by Laura De Pretto, Gloria Macri, and Catherine Wong. Leiden, Netherlands: Brill.

Haynes, John. 1893a. "The Woman's Vote Craze." Letter to the Editor. *Sydney Morning Herald* [NSW], November 11.

Haynes, John. 1893b. "The Woman's Vote Craze." Letter to the Editor. *Sydney Morning Herald* [NSW], November 24.

Hearn, Mark. 2000. "Hard Cash: John Dwyer and his Contemporaries, 1890–1914." PhD diss. University of Sydney.

Hearn, Mark. 2003. "Review of *Messages from Beyond: Spiritualism and Spiritualists in Melbourne's Golden Age, 1870–1890* by Alfred J. Gabay." *Labour History* 85:256–257.

Hearn, Mark. 2004. "Rose Summerfield's Gospel of Discontent: A Narrative of Radical Identity in Late Nineteenth Century Australia." *Labour History* 87:65–82.

Hearn, Mark. 2005. "Summerfield, Rose Anna (1864–1922)." *Australian Dictionary of Biography*, Supp. Volume. Carlton, VIC: University of Melbourne Press. https://adb.anu.edu.au/biography/summerfield-rose-anna-1582 (October 12, 2021).

Hearn, Mark, and Harry Knowles. 2004. "Struggling for Recognition: Reading the Individual in Labour History." *Labour History* 87:1–10.

Higham, Nick. 2006. "Paraguay is Providing England's Opponents in the Football World Cup Today. But Nick Higham Discovers that the Country has its own Trophy." *Independent* [London], June 10.

Hoare, Eileen. 2006. "The New Woman in the New World: Ibsen in Australia 1889–1891." Paper presented at the Conference of the Australasian Association for Drama, Theatre and Performance Studies, Department of Performance Studies, University of Sydney. https://ses.library.usyd.edu.au/handle/2123/2503?show=full (February 9, 2021).

Holland, H. E. 1920. "An Extremist of Yesterday: Some Memories of the Past." *Maoriland Worker* [Christchurch, N.Z.], February 11.

"How Does It Work?" 1920. *Rock Island Argus* [Illinois], April 2.

Huf, Elizabeth. 2010. "Great Shearers' Strike of 1891." *Queensland Historical Atlas*. https://www.qhatlas.com.au/content/great-shearers%E2%80%99-strike-1891 (December 21, 2020).

Iacovetta, Franca, Michael Quinlan, and Ian Radforth. 1996. "Immigration and Labour: Australia and Canada Compared." *Labour History* 71:90–115.

"Impracticability of Socialism." 1892. *Evening News* [Sydney, NSW], July 13.

"Insolvency." 1864. *Freeman's Journal* [Sydney, NSW], October 29.

"Intercolonial News: New South Wales." 1895. *Barrier Miner* [Broken Hill, NSW], February 2.

"In the Bush." 1893. *Worker* [Wagga, NSW], September 2.

"In the Supreme Court of New South Wales, Ecclesiastical Jurisdiction. In the Will of Henry Lewis Summerfield, late of Waverley, near Sydney, in the Colony of New South Wales, Gentleman, Deceased." 1890. *New South Wales Government Gazette* [Sydney, NSW], April 22.

"I.O.G.T." 1896. *Daily Telegraph* [Sydney, NSW], March 9.

Isaacs, Victor. 2015. "An Australian Newspaper in Paraguay 1894–1904." Canberra, ACT: Australian Society for the Study of Labour History. https://labourhistorycanberra.org/2015/05/an-australian-newspaper-in-paraguay-1894-1904/ (August 24, 2020).

James, Bob. 1986. "Anarchism and State Violence in Sydney and Melbourne 1886–1896." http://www.takver.com/history/aasv/index.htm (October 8, 2020).

James, Bob. 1999. "Larry Petrie (1859–1901)—Australian Revolutionist?" http://www.takver.com/history/petrie.htm (January 1, 2021).

James, Henry. [1878] 1966. "Daisy Miller." In *Great Short Works of Henry James* by Henry James. New York: Harper & Row.

Jones, Gareth Stedman. 1983. *Languages of Class: Studies in English Working Class History 1832–1982*. Cambridge, U.K.: Cambridge University Press.

Jullien, Dominique. 2005. "A Note on the Translation." In *Germinal* by Émile Zola, translated by Havelock Ellis. New York: Barnes & Noble.

Kellett, John. 1997. "William Lane and 'New Australia': A Reassessment." *Labour History* 72:1–18.

Kropotkin, Peter. [1899] 1912. *Fields, Factories and Workshops: Or, Industry Combined with Agriculture and Brain Work with Manual Work*. London: Nelson.

Kropotkin, Peter. [1906] 1990. *The Conquest of Bread.* Montréal: Black Rose.

Kropotkin, Peter. 1924. *Ethics: Origin and Development.* Translated by Louis S. Friedland and Joseph R. Piroshnikoff. New York: Dial.

"Labor Meeting at Cooma." 1892. *Daily Telegraph* [Sydney, NSW], December 20.

Lake, Marilyn, and Henry Reynolds. 2008. *Drawing the Global Colour Line: White Men's Countries and the Question of Racial Equality*. Melbourne, VIC: Melbourne University Press.

Lane, E. H. [1939] 1993. *Dawn to Dusk: Reminiscences of a Rebel*. Brisbane, QLD: Social History of Australia Publishing Enterprise.

Lane, William [as "John Miller"]. [1892] 2005. *The Workingman's Paradise: An Australian Labour Novel*. Chapel Hill, NC: Project Gutenberg.

Lansbury, Coral. 1967. "William Guthrie Spence." *Labour History* 13:3–10.

"Late Country News." 1892. *Sydney Mail* [NSW], October 8.

Laurie, Alderman A. 1938. "The Shearers' and Bushworkers' Strike of 1891." Paper presented at a meeting of the Historical Society of Queensland, October 25. UQ eSpace, University of Queensland.

Leach, Michael. 2002. "Don Eduardo Is Sleeping: A Return to New Australia, Paraguay." *Overland*, Summer.

"Lecture at New Lambton." 1893. *Newcastle Morning Herald and Miners' Advocate* [NSW], June 28.

"Lecture: Mrs. Cadogan on 'Flowers.'" 1899. *Worker* [Wagga, NSW], February 25.

"Lectures: Marvels of Ancient Peru." 1895. *Sydney Morning Herald* [NSW], July 10.

"Lectures: Socialism." 1893. *Newcastle Morning Herald and Miners' Advocate* [NSW], June 24.

"Letters from Paraguay." 1894. *Kiama Independent and Shoalhaven Advertiser* [Kiama, NSW], February 15.

"Let the Women Be Heard." 1894. *Worker* [Wagga, NSW], January 27.

Levey, Geoffrey Brahm. 2019. "Australia's 'Liberal Nationalist' Multiculturalism." In *Multiculturalism in the British Commonwealth: Comparative Perspectives on Theory and Practice*, editor by Richard T. Ashcroft and Mark Bevir. Berkeley: University of California Press.

Livermore, Harold V. 1950. "New Australia." *Hispanic American Historical Review* 30:290–313.

"Local & General." 1892. *Western Herald* [Bourke, NSW], September 10.

"Local & General." 1894. *Temuka Leader* [Canterbury, N.Z.], October 20.

Lyptus, Yuka. 1892. "Country Notes." *Goulburn Evening Penny Post* [NSW], November 19.

M. 1893. Letter to the Editor. *Sydney Morning Herald* [NSW], November 21.

Maley, Charles. 1897. "Ben Tillett and the Mayor." Letter to the Editor. *Barrier Miner* [Broken Hill, NSW], September 8.

"Man and Master." 1892. *Evening News* [Sydney, NSW], July 20.

"Manifesto to Bush Unions." 1894. *Maryborough Chronicle* [QLD], June 26.

Markus, Andrew. 1985. "Explaining the Treatment of Non-European Immigrants in Nineteenth Century Australia." *Labour History* 48:86–91.

"'Marriage and Social Life': Lecture by Miss Rose Scott." 1892. *Australian Star* [Sydney, NSW], April 25.

Martyn, T. 1926. "Paraguay: A Communistic Try-Out." *Evening News* [Rockhampton, QLD], December 27.

Marx, Karl. [1844] 1932. "Estranged Labor." In *Economic and Philosophical Manuscripts of 1844*. Moscow: Progress. https://www.marxists.org/archive/marx/works/1844/manuscripts/labour.htm (February 28, 2021).

"Mary Gilmore Tells of Cosme." 1952. *Tribune* [Sydney, NSW], November 5.

Mawson, Stephanie. 2011. "The 'Workingman's Paradise,' White Supremacy and Utopianism: The New Australia Movement and Working-Class Racism." *Labour History* 101:91–104.

McIlroy, Jim. 2003. *Australia's First Socialists*. Broadway, NSW: Resistance Books.

McKernan, Michael. 2012. "Down Under in Paraguay." Review of *Ticket to Paradise: A Journey to Find the Australian Colony in Paraguay among Nazis, Mennonites and Japanese Beekeepers*, by Ben Stubbs. *Sydney Morning Herald* [NSW], June 2.

McNaught, Peter. 1894. "Lane's Message." Letter to the Editor. *Worker* [Wagga, NSW], June 23.

"Merewether: Lecture." 1893. *Newcastle Morning Herald and Miners' Advocate* [NSW], June 29.

Merrett, Ian A. 1969. "A Reappraisal of the 1890 Maritime Strike in New Zealand." MA thesis. University of Canterbury [N.Z.].

"Miss Rose Scott: Hon. Secretary of the Womanhood Suffrage League of New South Wales." 1894. *Worker* [Wagga, NSW], January 6.

Molesworth, Voltaire "Vol." 1926. "Leon Cadogan's Plea to Australia." *Smith's Weekly* [Sydney, NSW], July 31.

"Mr. Hector Bolitho: Journalists' Welcome." 1934. *Auckland Star* [N.Z.], May 5.

"Mr. Herman Heberle: His Release from Gaol." 1893. *Barrier Miner* [Broken Hill, NSW], April 29.

"Mr. Joseph Symes." 1889. *Mercury and Weekly Courier* [Fitzroy, VIC], March 27.

"Mr. Rae, M.P., on Boycotting." 1892. *Telegraph* [Brisbane, QLD], December 28.

"Mrs. Ashton Again." 1892. *Daily Telegraph* [Sydney, NSW], April 11.

"Mrs. Rose Summerfield." 1892. *Worker* (Wagga, NSW], September 24.

"Mrs. Rose Summerfield: 'The Gospel of Discontent.'" 1892. *Western Herald* [Bourke, NSW], October 5.

"Mr. Tytherleigh's Candidature." 1894a. *Sydney Morning Herald* [NSW], July 14.

"Mr. Tytherleigh's Candidature." 1894b. *Sydney Morning Herald* [NSW], July 17.

Nelson, Garrett Dash. 2019. "The Splendor of Our Public and Common Life." *Places Journal*, December. https://placesjournal.org/article/edward-bellamy-urban-planning/?cn-relo&cn-reloaded=1 (December 8, 2021).

"New Australia." 1894a. *Temuka Leader* [Canterbury, N.Z.], March 13.

"New Australia." 1894b. *Temuka Leader* [Canterbury, N.Z.], March 31.

"New Australia." 1894c. *Temuka Leader* [Canterbury, N.Z.], May 5.

"New Australia." 1894d. *Temuka Leader* [Canterbury, N.Z.], May 22.

"New Australia." 1894e. *Temuka Leader* [Canterbury, N.Z.], July 17.

"New Australia." 1893. *Thames Advertiser* [Waikato, N.Z.], November 23.

"New Australia." 1894. *Western Champion* [Parkes, NSW], April 17.

"New Australia." 1927. *Windsor and Richmond Gazette* [Windsor, NSW], September 9.

"New Australia: Another Batch of Immigrants." 1893. *Auckland Star* [N.Z.], November 21.

"New Australia: Arrival of the Pioneers: A Second Detachment." 1893. *Star* [Christchurch, N.Z.], December 4.

"New Australia: Arrival of the Royal Tar." 1895. *Australian Star* [Sydney, NSW], January 19.

"New Australia: Career of the Rayol [*sic*] Tar." 1923. *Hokitika Guardian* [N.Z.], July 21.

"'New Australia' Expedition: First Contingent Sailed." 1893. *Auckland Star* [N.Z.], July 17.

"New Australia: Fresh Departure to the Settlement." 1895. *Wagga Advertiser* [NSW], March 19.

"'New Australia' in Paraguay." 1895. *British Australasian* [London, U.K.], August 1.

"New Australia: News from Paraguay." 1893. *Australian Star* [Sydney, NSW], December 21.

"New Australia: Settlement News." 1894. *Australian Star* [Sydney, NSW], March 20.

"New Australia's Part." 1916. *Tweed Daily* [Murwillumbah, NSW], September 17.

"New Factory Legislation: In Victoria." 1897. *Worker* [Brisbane, QLD], April 17.

"New Paraguay." 1916. *Macleay Chronicle* [Kempsey, NSW], September 20.

"News from Paraguay." 1903. *Worker* [Wagga, NSW], June 13.

"News of the Week." 1893. *Australian Town and Country Journal* [Sydney, NSW], June 24.

"New South Wales." 1892. *Telegraph* [Brisbane, QLD], December 20.

"New South Wales Mems." 1892. *Albury Banner and Wodonga Express* [Albury, NSW], December 30.

Nicol, W. 1979. "Women and the Trade Union Movement in New South Wales: 1890–1900." *Labour History* 36:18–30.

Nicole, Robert E. 2006. "Disturbing History: Aspects of Resistance in Early Colonial Fiji, 1874–1914." PhD diss. University of Canterbury [N.Z.].

Nicole, Robert E. 2011. *Disturbing History: Resistance in Early Colonial Fiji*. Honolulu: University of Hawai'i Press.

"Notes and Comments." 1897. *Worker* [Wagga, NSW], October 2.

"Notes and Comments." 1898. *Worker* [Wagga, NSW], November 12.

"Odd Colony in Paraguay." 1905. *Kennewick Courier* [Washington], September 22.

O'Lincoln, Tom. N.d. "Capital versus Labour: Australian Unions: From the Gold Rush to Arbitration." https://sa.org.au/interventions/aftergold.htm (October 7, 2020).

O'Sullivan, T. J. 1929. "The Passing of Leigh House." *Worker* [Brisbane, QLD], July 17.

"Outrage on the Aramac." 1893. *Bendigo Advertiser* [VIC], July 29.

Overacker, Louise. 1949. "The Australian Labor Party." *American Political Science Review* 43:677–703.

Painter, Alison. N.d. "29 May 1893: 'New Australia' in Paraguay." http://www.sahistorians.org.au/175/chronology/may/29-may-1893-new-australia-inparaguay.shtml (August 24, 2020).

"Paraguay Settlement." 1894. Editorial. *Kadina and Wallaroo Times* [Kadina, SA], April 11.
"Paraguay: The Cosme Settlement." 1895. *Australian Town and Country Journal* [Sydney, NSW], July 13.
Paroo's Offsider. 1892. "Here and There in the Back Country." *Hummer* [Wagga, NSW], October 8.
Parsons, Lucy E. 2004. *Freedom, Equality, & Solidarity: Writings & Speeches, 1878–1937.* Edited by Gale Ahrens. Chicago: Charles H. Kerr.
Parry, Naomi. 1997. "Review of *Paradise Mislaid: In Search of the Australian Tribe of Paraguay* by Anne Whitehead." Australian Society for the Study of Labour History. https://www.labourhistory.org.au/hummer/vol-3-no-2/paradise-mislaid/ (August 24, 2020).
Pascal, Blaise. [1670] 1849. *Pascal's Thoughts.* Translated by Rev. Edward Craig. Boston: Gould, Kendall and Lincoln.
Pearson, Charles. 1893. *National Life and Character: A Forecast.* London: Macmillan.
Perez, Danae. 2016. "English and Language Shift in Paraguay's New Australia." *World Englishes* 35:160–176.
"Personal." 1893. *Leader* [Melbourne, VIC], November 18.
"Personal." 1917. *Waikato Times* [N.Z.], August 27.
Petrey, D. Sandy. 1969. "The Revolutionary Setting of *Germinal*." *French Review* 43:54–63.
"Pilgrims from Paraguay: More Disgusted New Australians." 1897. *Queensland Times* [Ipswich, QLD], August 21.
"Plattsburg." 1893. *Newcastle Morning Herald and Miners' Advocate* [NSW], June 24.
"Political." 1894. *Worker* [Brisbane, QLD], June 16.
"Port Salvation." 1883. *Age* [Melbourne, VIC], July 21.
"Princess's Theatre—A Doll's House." 1889a. *Age* [Melbourne, VIC], September 16.
"Princess's Theatre: 'A Doll's House.'" 1889b. *Argus* [Melbourne, VIC], September 16.
Prior, Robert. 1907. "New Australia in Paraguay." *Worker* [Brisbane, QLD], January 24.
"Queensland." 1891a. *South Australian Register* [Adelaide, SA], April 22.
"Queensland." 1891b. Editorial. *Sydney Mail* [NSW], June 20.
"Queensland Labourers' Union: Disaffection Among Bush Workers." 1893. Editorial. *Queenslander* [Brisbane, QLD], October 21.
Radi, Heather. 1990. "Windeyer, Lady Mary Elizabeth (1836–1912)." *Australian Dictionary of Biography*. http://adb.anu.edu.au/biography/windeyer-lady-mary-elizabeth-1059 (October 20, 2020).
Reeve, George G. 1926. "New Australia: Cosme and William Lane." *Windsor and Richmond Gazette* [Windsor, NSW], April 9.
Reich, Pauline C., and Atsuko Fukuda. 1976. "Japan's Literary Feminists: The 'Seito' Group." *Signs* 2:280–291.
"Relieved from the Tax Man." 1900. *Evening Times* [Washington, DC], October 27.

"Return of the Royal Tar: Arrangements for a Shipment of Women." 1894. *Marlborough Express* [N.Z.], May 2.
"Rose Summerfield." N.d. https://en.wikipedia.org/wiki/Rose_Summerfield (November 26, 2020).
Ross, Lloyd. 1947. "The Philosophy of the Australian Labor Party." *Antioch Review* 7:109–124.
Saguier, Rubén Bareiro. 1979. "Paraguay—Culture of Fear." *Index on Censorship* 8:26–32.
Scates, Bruce. 1986. "'Millenium or Pandemonium?': Radicalism in the Labour Movement, Sydney, 1889-1899." *Labour History* 50:72–94.
Scates, Bruce. 1990. "Socialism, Feminism and the Case of William Lane: A Reply to Marilyn Lake." *Labour History* 59:45–58.
Schwarz, Kirrily. 2016. "Australia's Bizarre Socialist Colony in Paraguay." *Advertiser* [Adelaide, SA], October 17.
Scott, Rose [as "R.S."]. 1892a. "On Woman Suffrage." *Hummer* [Wagga, NSW], April 23.
Scott, Rose [as "R.S."]. 1892b. "Our Sisters' Column." *Hummer* [Wagga, NSW], July 2.
Scott, Rose. 1892c. Letter to the Editor. *Hummer* [Wagga, NSW], August 27.
Scott, Rose [as "R.S."]. 1892d. "Why Women Should Vote." *Hummer* [Wagga, NSW], July 30.
"Section—The Great 1889 Dockers' Strike." 2001. https://www.tuc.org.uk/research-analysis/reports/section-great-1889-dockers-strike (November 8, 2020).
Semmler, Clement. 1969. "Some Notes on the Literature of the Shearers' Strikes of 1891 and 1894." *Australian Quarterly* 41:75–87.
Shelley, Percy Bysshe. 1819. "The Mask of Anarchy: Written on the Occasion of the Massacre at Manchester." http://knarf.english.upenn.edu/PShelley/anarchy.html (January 28, 2021).
Shelley, Percy Bysshe. 1819–1820. "Lines Written During the Castlereagh Administration." https://verse.press/poem/lines-written-during-the-castlereagh-12402 (January 28, 2021).
"Shelley's Centenary: Celebration at the School of Arts." 1892. *Australian Star* [Sydney, NSW], August 5.
Shone, Steve J. 2010. *Lysander Spooner: American Anarchist*. Lanham, MD: Lexington.
Shone, Steve J. 2013. *American Anarchism*. Leiden, Netherlands: Brill.
Shone, Steve J. 2019. *Women of Liberty*. Leiden, Netherlands: Brill.
"Single-Tax League." 1895. *Sydney Morning Herald* [NSW], March 14.
"Sir John Robertson." 1895. *Albury Banner and Wodonga Express* [Albury, NSW], February 8.
Smith, F. B. 1963. "Joseph Symes and the Australasian Secular Association." *Labour History* 5:26–47.
Smith, F. B. 1976. "Joseph Symes (1841–1906)." In *Australian Dictionary of Biography*, vol. 6. Melbourne: Melbourne University Press.

Smith, Maud Violet Angelina. 1892. Letter to the Editor. *Hummer* [Wagga, NSW], July 23.

"Smoke Ho!" 1893a. *Worker* [Wagga, NSW], June 10.

"Smoke Ho!" 1893b. *Worker* [Wagga, NSW], June 24.

"Socialist Conference." 1892. *Evening News* [Sydney, NSW], December 26.

"Socialistic Colonies." 1894. Editorial. *Temuka Leader* [Canterbury, N.Z.], May 22.

"Socialist League." 1892. *Evening News* [Sydney, NSW], October 4.

"Socialists—Mrs. Rose Summerfield." 1892. *Evening News* [Sydney, NSW], August 26.

"SOCIALIST Sunday Evening Lectures." 1892. *Australian Star* [Sydney, NSW], August 27.

"Social to Mrs. Cadogan." 1899. *Worker* [Wagga, NSW], April 1.

"Some Good Points of Paraguay and New Australia." 1897. *Albury Banner and Wodonga Express* [Albury, NSW], January 15.

Souter, Gavin. [1968] 2012. *A Peculiar People: The Australians in Paraguay*. Digital edition. Sydney, NSW: Xoum.

Sparrow, Jeff, and Jill Sparrow. 2001. *Radical Melbourne: A Secret History*. Carlton North, VIC: Vulgar Press.

Spence, William G. 1893. "Secretary's Report: To the Members." *Shearers' and General Laborers' Record*, March 15.

Spooner, Lysander. [1852] 1971. *An Essay on the Trial by Jury.* In *The Collected Works of Lysander Spooner* by Lysander Spooner, ed. Charles Shively. 6 vols. Weston, MA: M & S.

Stanton, Elizabeth Cady. 1868. "Brick Pomeroy on the Situation." *Revolution*, December 17.

Stenhouse, John. 1993. "Collins, William Whitehouse." *Dictionary of New Zealand Biography*. https://teara.govt.nz/en/biographies/2c27/collins-william-whitehouse (January 19, 2021).

Stewart, Neil. 1972. "The Queensland Pastoral Strike of 1891." M.A. thesis. University of Queensland.

"St. Mary's Cathedral." 1893. *Daily Telegraph* [Sydney, NSW], April 6.

"Stone, Joseph." 1928. *Northern Territory Times* [Darwin, NT], July 13.

Stubbs, Ben. 2012. "The New Australians of South America." *Australian Geographic*, March/April.

Sullivan, Rodney J. 1979. "Casey, Gilbert Stephen (1856–1946)." *Australian Dictionary of Biography*. https://adb.anu.edu.au/biography/casey-gilbert-stephen-5528/text9415 (February 6, 2021).

Sullivan, Rodney J., and R. A. Sullivan. 1983. "The Pastoral Strikes, 1891 and 1894." In *The Big Strikes: Queensland 1889–1965*, ed. D. J. Murphy. St. Lucia: University of Queensland Press.

Summerfield, Rose. 1892a. "Co Operation." Letter to the Editor. *Gundagai Times* [NSW], November 25.

Summerfield, Rose. 1892b. "Master and Man." Address to the Australian Socialist League, July 17. https://www.reasoninrevolt.net.au/bib/PR0000099.htm (August 27, 2020).

Summerfield, Rose [as "Rose Hummer"]. 1892c. "Our Sisters' Column." *Hummer* [Wagga, NSW], July 30.

Summerfield, Rose [as "Rose Hummer"]. 1892d. "Our Sisters' Column." Letter to the Editor. *Hummer* [Wagga, NSW], August 13.

Summerfield, Rose [as "Rose Hummer"]. 1892e. "Our Sisters' Column." Letter to the Editor. *Hummer* [Wagga, NSW], August 27.

Summerfield, Rose [as "Rose Hummer"]. 1892f. "Our Sisters' Column." *Hummer* [Wagga, NSW], October 8.

Summerfield, Rose [as "Rose Hummer"]. 1892g. "Our Sisters' Column." *Hummer* [Wagga, NSW], October 29.

Summerfield, Rose [as "Rose Hummer"]. 1892h. "Our Sisters' Column: Australian Workers' Union." *Hummer* [Wagga, NSW], November 26.

Summerfield, Rose [as "Rose Hummer"]. 1892i. "Our Sisters' Column: The War of the Roses." *Hummer* [Wagga, NSW], September 3.

Summerfield, Rose. 1893a. "Protection of Young Girls." Letter to the Editor. *Daily Telegraph* [Sydney, NSW], November 28.

Summerfield, Rose. 1893b. "Resume of My Work in Connection with the General Laborers' Union, commencing 1 August 1892." *Shearers' and General Laborers' Record*, March 15.

Summerfield, Rose [as "Rose Hummer"]. 1893c. "Our Sisters' Column: Labor in Melbourne." *Hummer* [Wagga, NSW], March 25.

Summerfield, Rose. 1893d. "The Woman's Vote Craze." *Sydney Morning Herald* [NSW], November 24.

Summerfield, Rose. 1895a. "A Few Hours in Sydney Streets." 1895. *Worker* [Brisbane, QLD], September 7.

Summerfield, Rose. 1895b. "A Picture." *Australian Workman* [Sydney, NSW], August 3.

Summerfield, Rose. 1895c. "Women's Rights." *Worker* [Brisbane, QLD], November 2.

Summerfield, Rose. 1896a. "A Sermon in Stones." *Worker* [Brisbane, QLD], November 7.

Summerfield, Rose. 1896b. "Christmas, 1896." *Worker* [Brisbane, QLD], December 19.

Summerfield, Rose. 1896c. "Notes." *Worker* [Brisbane, QLD], January 11.

Summerfield, Rose. 1896d. "The Earth is the Lord's and the Fullness Thereof." *Worker* [Brisbane, QLD], October 31.

Summerfield, Rose. 1897. "A Few Scraps of Ben Tillett's Life and Thoughts." *Worker* [Brisbane, QLD], August 21.

Summerfield, Rose [as "Rose Cadogan"]. 1898a. "An Election Appeal." *Worker* [Wagga, NSW], July 23.

Summerfield, Rose [as "Rose Cadogan"]. 1898b. "Be True to Self." *Worker* [Wagga, NSW], May 28.

Summerfield, Rose [as "Rose Cadogan"]. 1898c. "Branded Children." *Worker* [Wagga, NSW], April 16.

Summerfield, Rose [as "R. C."]. 1898d. "Branded Children." Letter to the Editor. *Worker* [Wagga, NSW], May 7.

Summerfield, Rose [as "Rose Cadogan"]. 1898e. "Dreams and Seems." *Worker* [Wagga, NSW], August 27.

Summerfield, Rose [as "Rose Cadogan"]. 1898f. "Here and Now." *Worker* [Wagga, NSW], January 22.

Summerfield, Rose [as "Rose Cadogan"]. 1898g. "Love of Comrades." *Worker* [Brisbane, QLD], April 23.

Summerfield, Rose [as "Rose Cadogan"]. 1898h. "My Baptism." *Worker* [Wagga, NSW], July 2.

Summerfield, Rose [as "Rose Cadogan"]. 1898i. "Not True." *Worker* [Wagga, NSW], February 5.

Summerfield, Rose [as "Rose Cadogan"]. 1898j. "Present Day Problems." *Worker* [Wagga, NSW], November 19.

Summerfield, Rose [as "R. C.]. 1898k. "Stray Notes." *Worker* [Wagga, NSW], September 3.

Summerfield, Rose [as "Rose Cadogan"]. 1898l. "Sympathy." *Worker* [Wagga, NSW], June 4.

Summerfield, Rose [as "Rose Cadogan"]. 1898m. "The Need of the Hour." *Worker* [Wagga, NSW], January 15.

Summerfield, Rose [as "Rose Cadogan"]. 1898n. "The Politician." *Worker* [Wagga, NSW], January 29.

Summerfield, Rose [as "Rose Cadogan"]. 1898o. "There's Always Good in Work." *Worker* [Wagga, NSW], July 30.

Summerfield, Rose [as "Rose Cadogan"]. 1898p. "The Union Label: What Women Can Do." *Worker* [Wagga, NSW], May 14.

Summerfield, Rose [as "Rose Cadogan"]. 1898q. "The Union Label: What Women Can Do (Continued)." *Worker* [Wagga, NSW], May 21.

Summerfield, Rose [as "Rose Cadogan"]. 1898r. "True Womanhood." *Worker* [Wagga, NSW], June 18.

Summerfield, Rose [as "Rose Cadogan"]. 1898s. "Unionism." *Worker* [Wagga, NSW], February 19.

Summerfield, Rose [as "Rose Cadogan"]. 1899a. "Reason Versus Sentiment." *Worker* [Wagga, NSW], January 28.

Summerfield, Rose [as "Rose Cadogan"]. 1899b. "Stray Notes." *Worker* [Wagga, NSW], February 18.

Summerfield, Rose [as "Rose Cadogan"]. 1915. "Australia." *Worker* [Brisbane, QLD], March 11.

"Supreme Court: Criminal Jurisdiction." 1891a. *Morning Bulletin* [Rockhampton, QLD], May 4.

"Supreme Court: Criminal Jurisdiction." 1891b. *Morning Bulletin* [Rockhampton, QLD], May 16.

Svensen, Stuart. 1995. *The Sinews of War: Hard Cash and the 1890 Maritime Strike.* Sydney: University of New South Wales Press.

"Sydney." 1892. *Maryborough Chronicle* [QLD], December 31.

Symes, Peter. 2004. "The Notes of New Australia." http://www.pjsymes.com.au/ (August 31, 2020).
Tarnoff, Ben. 2011. "Magical Thinking." *Lapham's Quarterly*, Fall.
"Telegrams." 1894. *Temuka Leader* [Canterbury, N.Z.], October 20.
"The Aramac Explosion." 1893. *Newcastle Morning Herald and Miners' Advocate* [NSW], July 29.
"The Art Society." 1894. *Daily Telegraph* [Sydney, NSW], August 4.
"The Broken Hill Miners: A Strike Impending." 1892. *Bathurst Free Press and Mining Journal* [NSW], July 4.
"The Broken Hill Miners' Strike: Interview with Mr. Sleath." 1892. *Sydney Morning Herald* [NSW], July 27.
"The Broken Hill Prosecutions." 1892. Editorial. *Windsor and Richmond Gazette* [Windsor, NSW], November 5.
"The Broken Hill Sentences." 1892. *Evening News* [Sydney, NSW], October 31.
"The Broken Hill Strike." 1892a. Editorial. *Burra Record* [SA], September 21.
"The Broken Hill Strike." 1892b. Editorial. *Evening Journal* [Adelaide, SA], August 22.
"The Bush Strike." 1891. *Warwick Argus* [QLD], June 13.
"The Bush Workers." 1891. Editorial. *Queenslander* [Brisbane, QLD], April 11.
"The Bush Workers." 1892. Editorial. *Queenslander* [Brisbane, QLD], March 26.
"The Cadogans in Exile." 1902. *Worke*r [Wagga, NSW], August 30.
"The Chicago Anarchists." 1898. *Worke*r [Wagga, NSW], November 19.
"The Colony at Cosme: Progress of the English Community in Paraguay." 1901. *English Lakes Visitor* [U.K.], September 28.
"The Conspiracy Trial at Rockhampton." 1891. *Argus* [Melbourne, VIC], May 20.
"The Cosme Colony: Lecture in Gloucester." 1897. *Gloucester Journal* [U.K.], March 13.
"The Explosion on the Aramac." 1893. *Argus* [Melbourne, VIC], August 12.
The Flaneur. 1895. "Acta Populi." *Freeman's Journal* [Sydney, NSW], April 13.
"The Grafter's Wallet." 1901. *Worker* [Wagga, NSW], November 23.
"The Labor Deserters." 1892. *Evening News* [Sydney, NSW], October 6.
"The Labor Difficulty at Broken-Hill: Miners' Mass Meeting." 1892. *Daily Telegraph* [Sydney, NSW], May 21.
"The Labor Platform." 1894. *Daily Telegraph* [Sydney, NSW], June 11.
"The Late Mr. William Lane." 1917. *New Zealand Herald* [Auckland], August 27.
"The Latest Utopia: A 'Looking Backward' Town." 1905. *Leeds Mercury* [U.K.], June 24,
"The Miners' Strike at Broken Hill." 1892. *Argus* [Melbourne, VIC], October 31.
"The New Australia." 1894. *Temuka Leader* [Canterbury, N.Z.], March 29.
"The New Australia: Paraguay and Cosme." 1924. *Toowoomba Chronicle and Darling Downs Gazette* [Toowoomba, QLD], May 23.
"The New Australia Scheme: The Settlement at Paraguay." 1893. *Northern Star* (Lismore, NSW], June 14.
"The New Australia Settlement." 1893. *Argus* [Melbourne, VIC], October 5.

"The New Australia Settlement: Safe Arrival at Paraguay." 1893. *Tasmanian News* [Hobart], October 5.
"The 'New Australia' Settlement in Paraguay." 1893. *Brisbane Courier* [QLD], July 4.
"The Pamphlet Collection of Sir Robert Stout: Volume 82." N.d. New Zealand Electronic Text Collection. http://nzetc.victoria.ac.nz/tm/scholarly/Stout82-fig-Stout82P013019a.html (January 18, 2021).
"The Paraguay Temperance Settlement." 1893. *Kadina and Wallaroo Times* [Kadina, SA], December 30.
"The Productive Property of Land." 1893. *Shearers' and General Laborers' Record*, June 15.
"The Queensland Shearers: Mr. Justice Harding on the Conspiracy Cases." 1891. *Freeman's Journal* [Sydney, NSW], May 30.
"The Queensland Strike." 1891. *Australian Star* [Sydney, NSW], April 20.
"The Sentenced Shearers." 1891. Editorial. *Bendigo Independent* [VIC], May 23.
"The Shearers' Dispute: The Rockhampton Trials." 1891. *Brisbane Courier* [QLD], May 19.
"The Shearing Difficulty: Work Proceeding Quietly." 1894. *Evening News* [Sydney, NSW], July 14.
"The Socialist Conference." 1892. *Evening News* [Sydney, NSW], December 31.
"The Socialist League." 1892. *Evening News* [Sydney, NSW], September 30.
"The Womanhood Suffrage League." 1893. *Dawn* [Sydney, NSW], September 1.
"The Workers' Ball." 1892. *Gundagai Times* [NSW], November 15.
"The Workers' Library Ball." 1892. *Gundagai Times* [NSW], September 13.
"The Workers' Union of N.S.W." 1892. *Gundagai Times* [NSW], November 11.
"The World of Labour." 1892. *Worker* [Brisbane, QLD], October 8.
Thompson, Stephen. 2013. "1893: The New Australia Colony Collection." University of Sydney Library, February. http://www.migrationheritage.nsw.gov.au/exhibition/objectsthroughtime/1893-the-new-australia-colony-collection/index.html (January 23, 2021).
"To the Editor." 1929. *Northern Territory Times* [Darwin, NT], December 6.
"Trade Affairs." 1892. *Evening News* [Sydney, NSW], August 25.
"Trades Movements." 1892a. *Sydney Morning Herald* [NSW], August 11.
"Trades Movements." 1892b. *Sydney Morning Herald* [NSW], August 25.
Tui. 1892. "Bird's-Eye View: From Sydney." *Hummer* [Wagga, NSW], July 23.
United Pastoralists' Association of Queensland. 1891. *The Great Queensland Strike of 1891*. Brisbane, QLD: Black, Keid.
Untitled. 1893. *Ballarat Star* [VIC], February 13.
Untitled. 1920. *Ashburton Guardian* [N.Z.], April 23.
Vandelaar, Michael. 1985. "The Haymarket Affair 'Down Under.'" http://www.takver.com/history/aia/aia00001.htm (November 13, 2020).
Virdee, Satnam. 2017. "Socialist Antisemitism and its Discontents in England, 1884–98." *Patterns of Prejudice* 51:356–373.
"Waverley Womanhood Suffrage League." 1894. *Sydney Morning Herald* [NSW], September 13.

"Waverley Womanhood Suffrage League." 1895a. *Sydney Morning Herald* [NSW], January 5.

"Waverley Womanhood Suffrage League." 1895b. *Sydney Morning Herald* [NSW], March 4.

"Waverley Womanhood Suffrage League." 1895c. *Sydney Morning Herald* [NSW], June 10.

"Waverley Womanhood Suffrage League." 1895d. *Daily Telegraph* [Sydney, NSW], September 9.

"Waverley Womanhood Suffrage Social." 1895. *Daily Telegraph* [Sydney, NSW], July 18.

"Waverley Woman's Suffrage League." 1895. *Sydney Morning Herald* [NSW], February 2.

W. G. 1895. "Cosme." *Worker* [Wagga, NSW], September 14.

Whitehead, Anne. [1997] 2018. *Paradise Mislaid: In Search of the Australian Tribe of Paraguay*. Digital edition. Brisbane, QLD: King Tide Publishing.

Whitehead, Anne. [2003] 2018. *Blue Stocking In Patagonia: Mary Gilmore's Quest for Love and Utopia at the World's End*. Digital edition. Brisbane, QLD: King Tide Publishing.

Whittier, John Greenleaf. [1843] 1997. "Anti-Slavery Poems: Songs of Labor and Reform." Ann Arbor, MI: University of Michigan Humanities Text Initiative. https://quod.lib.umich.edu/a/amverse/BAE0044.0001.001/1:5.5?rgn=div2;view=fulltext (February 9, 2021).

"Woe and Trouble in Australia." 1895. *Silver Blade* [Rathdrum, Idaho], June 15.

Wolstenholme, M. S. 1893. "The Woman's Vote." Letter to the Editor. *Sydney Morning Herald* [NSW], November 13.

"Woman and the Marriage Laws." 1892. *Daily Telegraph* [Sydney, NSW], April 11.

"Womanhood Suffrage." 1892. *Sydney Morning Herald* [NSW], July 13.

"Womanhood Suffrage." 1893. *Daily Telegraph* [Sydney, NSW], December 12.

"Womanhood Suffrage." 1894a. *Sydney Morning Herald* [NSW], March 3.

"Womanhood Suffrage." 1894b. *Sydney Morning Herald* [NSW], April 14.

"Womanhood Suffrage." 1894c. *Sydney Morning Herald* [NSW], July 7.

"Womanhood Suffrage." 1894d. *Sydney Morning Herald* [NSW], September 7.

"Womanhood Suffrage." 1895. *Evening News* [Sydney, NSW], January 5.

"Womanhood Suffrage." 1897. *Worker* [Wagga, NSW], October 23.

"Womanhood Suffrage: Addresses by Sir Henry Parkes and Mr. Bruce Smith." 1893. *Sydney Morning Herald* [NSW], November 9.

"Womanhood Suffrage League." 1892. *Evening News* [Sydney, NSW], March 11.

"Womanhood Suffrage League." 1893a. *Evening News* [Sydney, NSW], June 15.

"Womanhood Suffrage League." 1893b. *Dawn* [Sydney, NSW], July 1.

"Womanhood Suffrage League." 1893c. *Evening News* [Sydney, NSW], August 10.

"Womanhood Suffrage League." 1894a. *Sydney Morning Herald* [NSW], January 23.

"Womanhood Suffrage League." 1894b. *Cumberland Mercury* [Parramatta, NSW], July 28.

"Womanhood Suffrage: Meeting at Petersham." 1894. *Australian Star* [Sydney, NSW], February 27.

"Woman's Rights." 1892. *Singleton Argus* [NSW], June 8.
"Woman's Suffrage." 1893. *Singleton Argus* [NSW], November 11.
"Woman's Suffrage." 1894. *Evening News* [Sydney, NSW], January 24.
"Woman's Suffrage." 1895. *Sydney Morning Herald* [NSW], March 15.
"Woman's Suffrage: Waverley Branch Meeting." 1895. *Evening News* [Sydney, NSW], February 2.
"Woman Suffrage." 1895. *Daily Telegraph* [Sydney, NSW], June 10.
"Woman Suffrage: Address by Mr. Casey." 1895. *Daily Telegraph* [Sydney, NSW], January 5.
"Women's Suffrage." 1894. *Evening News* [Sydney, NSW], September 6.
"Women's Suffrage League." 1894. *Evening News* [Sydney, NSW], July 12.
"Women's Suffrage League: Three Lady Orators." 1893. *Evening News* [Sydney, NSW], November 9.
"Women's Suffrage Meeting." 1893. *Goulburn Herald* [NSW], November 10.
"Women's Work and Pay: Starvation Wages." 1893. *Shearers' and General Laborers' Record*, February 15.
Zola, Émile. [1894] 2005. *Germinal.* Translated by Havelock Ellis. New York: Barnes & Noble.

Index

About the Author

Steve J. Shone received his PhD in political science from the University of California-Riverside. He has taught at a number of colleges, including Winona State University, Gonzaga University, and the University of Texas-Rio Grande Valley. He is the author of *Lysander Spooner: American Anarchist* (Lexington Books, 2010), *American Anarchism* (Brill, 2013; paperback edition Haymarket Books, 2014), and *Women of Liberty* (Brill, 2019; paperback edition Haymarket Books, 2020). He was a contributor to *The SAGE Handbook of Human Trafficking and Modern Day Slavery* (2018).

www.ingramcontent.com/pod-product-compliance
Ingram Content Group UK Ltd.
Pitfield, Milton Keynes, MK11 3LW, UK
UKHW041840031026
15587UKWH00002B/896

9 781666 909401